Stepping Free of Limiting Patterns

by Pat McCallum

Source Unlimited
Chevy Chase, MD

© August 1992 by Patricia McCallum

All rights reserved. No part of this book may be used or reproduced in any manner whatsoever without written permission except in the case of brief quotations embodied in critical articles and reviews. For information, write Source Unlimited.

"Essence Repatterning" and "Source Unlimited" are trademarks of Patricia McCallum.

This book is manufactured in the United States of America.

Designed by Blaine Fairchild.

Cover design by Jim Haynes of Graphics Plus, Silver Spring, MD 20901.

Published by Source Unlimited
P.O. Box 15826
Chevy Chase, MD 20815

ISBN 0-9634488-0-3

Acknowledgements

I am grateful to the many dedicated, warm individuals with whom I have worked in *Essence Repatterning*™ sessions.

I thank the following people for their valuable contributions to producing this book: Stephen Beltz, Bill Cates, Jeff Davidson, Juan Deliz, Pam Dinkel, Judith Epstein, Rena Johnson, Patricia Jones, Gayle Kitchings, Torrie Mattes, Natalie Meeks, Larry Sagen, Andrea Scott, Julie Shapiro, and Barry Sultanoff.

Special thanks goes to Blaine Fairchild for book design, layout, and off-the-wall humor at just the right moment.

This book is dedicated to
the spirit and essence within each of us.

Introduction

Several summers ago, at the beach, I began what I know now was to be a journey of self-discovery and exploration that would go beyond anything I had done up until that time. That was the summer I first heard about the concept of *limiting patterns*.

At that point, I had read enough self-help books and taken enough growth trainings to know that *I* was the one who was holding me back. It wasn't the proverbial *them*, or *society*, or just bad *karma*. I had finally accepted my growing suspicion that it was I who was sabotaging my own best efforts to move forward. I sensed that if only I could get out of my own way, then things would be different. But what to do? There didn't seem to be any structured approach that did more than aim at specific issues in an effort to fix just those issues. Yes, some of these approaches worked, and I worked them. But inside I was asking, "What about the big picture, my whole life? How do I deal with that?" Although I didn't know what I was looking for, I did know that I was frustrated and stuck, sitting on my potential and waiting for my life to begin.

Obviously, every one of those approaches *did* work for me. Each of them helped me take my next step, and the one after that, and on and on. So it all had value, enormous value. Perhaps *you* can say the same thing. In fact, I would imagine that everything you have done up until now has prepared you for the approach outlined in these pages.

Looking back to that summer, I marvel at how much has evolved since then. When I happened upon the concept of limiting patterns, it was in a barebones way, i.e.: "Here is a way to remove *one* limiting pattern." I stress *one* pattern, because I have learned, through trial and error over the years, that each specific limiting pattern has so many permutations, literally dozens of them, that even if you learn how to remove *one* of them, you may not even notice it, because the rest of those permutations will still be in place.

However, back then, I was excited. First, just the *idea* of limiting patterns hinted to me of a framework, of a logical rationale, for what I perceived to be seemingly unrelated behaviors and experiences. Second, I was excited by the prospect of actually being able to remove *a* limiting pattern.

As I began experimenting, I found that the method I had read about was difficult and arduous. It required being able to access various parts of one's mind, and to establish communication within them, in order to do the technique properly. At that point, however, I didn't care. It was all I had, and I was grateful for it.

I soon learned to do the technique, and even became proficient at it. As I did, I found that it took me about three or four minutes to remove each pattern...a fact that became increasingly significant as I slowly began learning about the many *other* patterns, specifically related to the one being addressed, that were *not* being removed. (As an example, let's consider the issue of stress. I have learned that it is one thing to remove the experience of feeling stress in one's life, but that, alone, will *not* remove the separate patterns of *being* stressful...or *acting* stressful...or even *thinking* in stressful ways, just to name a few of the possible permutations of that particular pattern.)

As part of my exploration of ways that would assist me in moving forward, I had taken some seminars in *Three-in-One Concepts*, an innovative approach that teaches one how to more fully integrate and balance various parts of the brain and the body. In those seminars I learned how to use Applied Kinesiology, also known as muscle-testing, as a means of accessing direct feedback and information from the body. (I had first experienced Applied Kinesiology ten years earlier when my doctor used it to diagnose misalignments in my spine and to determine the proper treatment for me. See **Appendix A**.)

As I explored this new world of limiting patterns, I used Applied Kinesiology, muscle-testing myself, to identify the range of permutations for each pattern that had to be addressed in order to fully remove a particular, specifically-worded pattern.

However, in experimenting with this exciting new technique for removing limiting patterns, I found yet another drawback. In addition to the length of time it took to remove just one permutation of a particular pattern, and the demanding, inner focus required to do the process, I learned, early on, that it was a process that was difficult for many people to do themselves, even when guided. However, I persevered on my own, experimenting, and discovering more and more about limiting patterns.

During this process, I found that as I uncovered each subsequent layer of a pattern and removed it, it was as if I was continually emerging at the top of the next sand dune, seeing my life and my patterns from yet another, broader perspective. Step by step through the sand, often finding myself led up a blind pathway brought on by a false assumption, I continued tracing, and retracing, my steps, tracking and documenting my progress as I went.

At one point, I even learned about a somewhat easier way to remove limiting patterns. It used self-hypnosis and also required an ability to maintain a specific inner focus. I latched onto it, grateful for whatever would make the process easier. However, I found that even this easier approach was still difficult to guide others in doing.

Then, one day, sometime later, after using this latest version to clear out many, many of my limiting patterns, it was as if my creative juices conspired to show me a much easier way to do what I had been laboring to do for so long. That day, as I began to follow my standard procedure, it was as if a voice inside me suddenly said, "No. Don't do it that way. Do it this way...". In that moment, I heard how to remove limiting patterns in the simple, elegant way that has become the *Essence Repatterning*™ process. The process is one that anyone can do. It is straightforward and requires *no* inner focus or self-hypnosis.

Since that time, I have taught many people to do *Essence Repatterning* for themselves. This book is based upon their experiences plus the data I have gathered in working with individuals in private sessions, documenting the patterns removed and their subsequent changes. Presently the thrust of my work is shifting toward research on *Essence Repatterning* applications in group and organizational settings.

Essence Repatterning is specifically recommended for healthy individuals who want their lives to work better. I am not recommending it to those with psychiatric disorders, although there are medical doctors who are using it in controlled settings within their practices in psychiatric situations, and there are psychotherapists who are using it to create significant, rapid progress with their clients.

Essentially, *Essence Repatterning* is for those who know that...if they always *do* what they've always done, they'll always *get* what they've always gotten. In other words, *Essence Repatterning* is for those who know that if they want things to *be* different, then they have to *do* things differently.

One of the aspects of *Essence Repatterning* that appeals to me the most is its efficiency. It allows the user, with a minimum amount of effort, to effect a maximum amount of change. I value my time and energy—and I love being able to use both of these resources strategically.

One caution I offer as you begin experimenting with this process: Beware of shortcuts. That is, beware of any tendency to try and figure out a faster, more streamlined, way to remove all of the patterns you will be identifying. First of all, the process you will be learning *is* fast...and streamlined. Secondly, those shortcuts can slow you down, making you think you've reframed everything, when you haven't. I learned this lesson the hard way. Thirdly, I also learned that the ego often has an investment in undercutting the very thing that could change our lives the most.

Finally, I suggest that as you read, you take time to chew on the information and jot down any patterns you notice in a journal or notebook devoted specifically to that. The more thoughtful—and active—you are in your reading, the more you will get from it. This is not a book, or material, you will benefit from by racing through. In fact, the more patterns you identify—and remove, as directed—the more changes you will notice in yourself and your life by the time you have completed this book.

1

What If...

What if you could change the circumstances of your life... how you are treated by others...how you treat others...how you deal with money...how you feel about yourself and how confident you are?

Many, if not most people reading this book know or suspect that in some way their lives have been influenced, and perhaps even limited, by what they experienced and learned about life, as they were growing up.

Many readers may be, or have been, involved in self-help support groups, 12-Step programs, individual psychotherapy, and/or encounter groups. Although many people who are using this new process also participate in these and similar approaches, this book is about a method by which anyone, on his or her own, can begin stepping free of the limiting patterns learned as a child. It is a focused, easy-to-learn, practical approach that can be used daily to deal effectively with limiting patterns as they arise.

Standard of Living

What if you didn't have to settle for any semblance of life that is based on how you were raised...the standard of living your parents had...or the quality of relationship they had?

What if you didn't have to raise your children to feel the way *you* did as a child...treat your mate the way your parents treated one another...or, perhaps most importantly, treat yourself the way your parents or parent-figures treated you?

Sounds like magic, wishful thinking, or pure delusion, right?

What If You Could?

But what if it worked, and is working...over and over, for many people in many walks of life, regardless of race, creed, color, ethnic origin, physical abilities, or educational background?

If it *were* magic, you wouldn't know how the changes occurred. For magic is the word we use to describe those instances that occur once, or perhaps twice, but that seem to appear out of nowhere...something we hope will happen again, but which we have no idea how to initiate on our own.

Magic describes occurrences over which we seem to have no control...happenings that seem to take place outside ourselves, without input from us.

Wishful thinking, on the other hand, is familiar to all of us. It is focusing, or even obsessing, through hopes and dreams about what we want, without knowing what to do to make those wishes a reality—or perhaps being unwilling to do what it takes, even if someone told us how to do it.

Step-By-Step Changes

This book is about a process, a step-by-step technique, that individuals are using to change their lives in substantive ways. It is being used by some individuals who are very successful in most parts of their lives, but perhaps deficient in a few...and it is being used by others who are just learning to be successful and finding new ways to express who they are and how to interact effectively with the world.

This technique is being used successfully by travel agents, financial planners, marketing executives, housewives and mothers, lawyers, bank cashiers, couriers, medical doctors, artists, university administrators, psychotherapists, computer specialists, government workers, health-care professionals, trainers, entrepreneurs, physical therapists, bank tellers, accountants, secretaries, editors, aerobics instructors, realtors, political activists...and many others.

It is being used by people who have long felt isolated...or disconnected, from themselves and from those around them. It is being used by people who have felt at a deadend in their jobs—or in their relationships—unfulfilled, but not knowing which way to turn. It also is being used by people who have known they were blocked, but had felt as if they were stuck in a brown paper bag with no idea of how to find their way out.

Remove Limiting Patterns

Using this process, they have learned to identify the limiting patterns that give rise to these frustrating experiences, *remove these patterns*...and set a new direction. With this approach, they have learned how to actually create new inner pathways that result in different treatment on the job, in their relationships, and with their children.

Perhaps more importantly and fundamentally, those using this approach typically report that they feel more relaxed and at peace with themselves. They feel more in control of their lives and more confident. These changes are reflected in their home life, work, finances, and health—physical, mental, and emotional.

This approach is called *Essence Repatterning*™. It is an elegantly simple process for working directly with the negative messages stored in the subconscious. With this process you can remove these messages in a measured, timely fashion that is directed by your own inner knowing and unconscious. *Essence Repatterning* allows you to make only those changes that you can easily integrate—at a pace that is right for you.

Individual Experiences

To illustrate the range of applications for *Essence Repatterning*, here are some first-hand accounts:

• "Using *Essence Repatterning* is helping my travel business prosper—during a recession—and has helped me clear the track to buy the house I have long wanted. In the process, I have used repatterning to peel away layers of reactions and negative feelings that have long inhibited me from achieving my goals.

"As I look back over the months that I have been doing *Essence Repatterning*, I recall my first delightful success, last December while skiing in Colorado.

"When I first arrived on the ski slopes, I felt awkward, old (I'm 50), and fat. I realized that I don't like skiing poorly, and that falling down is not my idea of fun; I could be hurt. Rather than simply stew with all these negative feelings, later, back in my room, I started identifying some of my limiting patterns around skiing. What I found were many negative beliefs, feelings, and fears that not only related to skiing but also to many other areas of performance and achievement. Now I realize that by removing those patterns while skiing, I probably was supporting my general career goals as well.

"At any rate, after removing many, many patterns that day and throughout the week—I skied better than I ever have. It was easy, smooth, and great fun. Not only that, I felt great and looked good, too."

—N.B.M., travel agent, Washington, D.C.

• "When I heard a seminar leader say that she wasn't interested in anything that didn't 'grow corn', I was intrigued. Now I know that *Essence Repatterning does* grow corn, and grows it abundantly. The effects of using this process have been profound and far-reaching. For example, in my work as an association editor, I am taking care of myself in ways that, up until now,

I simply did not have the courage for—standing up for myself, speaking my truth, and saying what someone else may not want to hear, and letting the chips fall where they may. In general, I have found that my relationships are richer and more fulfilling because I am freer, easier, and more flexible.

"As a lifelong singer, I've attained goals which I feared were unattainable. My singing has improved remarkably. My range is the same, but the notes at each extreme are easier and fuller, even before the voice is warmed up. Even my sporadic piano playing has improved—without any additional practice.

"I've learned to drive a car after decades of dependency on others. I'm healthy, energetic, and have dropped unwanted weight. I even have an improved relationship with my environment. For decades, I felt ill every summer when I had to be out in high temperatures and humidity. Since I have worked with that as a limiting pattern, I am much better able to tolerate the summer heat.

"I have experienced support from people in ways that are brand-new for me. Unsolicited, people regularly have offered me rides and allowed me to drive their cars as I prepared for my driver's test. I even have received financial assistance to buy a new car from family members who formerly were firmly opposed to helping me out."

—J.H.E., publications editor, Reston, Va.

- "The most significant change I've noticed in myself since I began using *Essence Repatterning* is that I no longer feel overwhelmed; I no longer feel like giving up, as if I can't go on. Now, no matter how bad something might seem, I know it can be repatterned.

"For example, when I began using this process, I was addicted to overspending and my finances were chronically in the red. Now my money is going further, and I don't feel the pressure to buy. I don't *have* to have that new dress, or a new dining table, to feel worthwhile. In fact, I am finding that I don't worry much about money anymore and, if I do, I work with the limiting patterns that give rise to that worry.

"Another change I've noticed is that, as recently as eight months ago, I sometimes felt almost schizophrenic, trying to be a mother to my 6-year-old and 17-year-old, work a full-time job, and follow my personal interests. I felt scattered, and it seemed to take a lot of energy to shift out of one identity into another. At this point, my life is much more integrated, and I feel more centered. Now there is just *one* me that's doing all these different things.

"This change is reflected in my relationship with my daughters too. For instance, because I used to be a major worrier, I frequently was on the phone to my daughter who is away at college. Now I give her a lot more space, because I'm not obsessing about her so much. Also, by helping her work with her limiting patterns, she is making significant shifts too.

"Two major changes I've seen in my six-year-old is that she is generally more cooperative and articulate about her needs. This has made life much simpler for me. Now when she needs me, or wants to be close, she will say this, instead of just whining and leaving it for me to figure out what she needs.

"One of the results of my first *Essence Repatterning* session was that I began to realize that my dream of buying property, specifically rental property, was a real possibility. Today, I am in the process of finalizing that purchase.

"As I use *Essence Repatterning* each day, I am still struck by how simple and direct it is. I like knowing that dealing with my issues doesn't have to be hard work...or, for example, that I don't have to practice meditation two hours a day for 20 years to get results. The process is always available. I'm also finding that *whatever* I'm doing now, I'm more efficient and effective. The repatterning process seems to enhance everything, including my meditation."

—G.K., staff assistant, Washington, D.C.

- "Since I began working with *Essence Repatterning* almost nine months ago, I have experienced shifts in virtually every area of my life, but the most noticeable change is a sense of optimism and knowing that I am in charge of my life, and that I can create the results I want.

"In the area of my work as a psychotherapist, I no longer feel that I have to do it the way my father did: go in to the office, crank out the hours, struggle to make the bucks to pay the bills, and never really feel that there's ever enough. I have recognized my own lifelong patterns of struggle (similar to what I saw my father do) and have moved past them into a much more comfortable, easy relationship with my work, money, and time.

"I am *enjoying* my therapy sessions with clients much more; and my clients are getting results faster, even though it is all so much easier for me: instead of struggle and toil, there is a confident settling back into myself, trusting the moment, *knowing* that I have what it takes in each moment to get the job done.

"I also am having success in areas that heretofore had eluded me. For example, I'm now utilizing long-dormant skills in math to make wise and profitable investments. Since I began using *Essence Repatterning*, I have actually generated more *passive* income through investments than I have earned working in my medical office. This is a total departure from any other time in my life, as my previous pattern had been always to come out a financial loser, time and time again.

"Another specific area in which I have seen major changes is in my career. Rather than feeling limited by a rather linear approach of only seeing individual clients, I have been going for more of what I *really* want, which is to present myself more publicly as a speaker and workshop facilitator.

"For the first time ever, I have overcome patterns of fearing public exposure (believing that I'd be discredited, humiliated, etc.) and am feeling confident that I can be *publicly* who I am. I am completing a professional promotional packet, in which I am presenting much more of the truth of who I am and what I stand for. There is now much more congruence between who I know myself to be *inside* (my values, my dreams and visions, etc.) and the way I'm choosing to be seen.

"In relationships, I've largely moved past old patterns of being a kind of 'sensitive guy', always trying to be nice and accommodating. I'm now having relationships that are much more on my terms—choosing and creating friendships and intimate relationships that are fulfilling and in depth, without having to distort my expression in order to get what I want.

"A core pattern for me throughout my life has been to believe that I am not enough. Along with that have been patterns of being very self-critical and focusing heavily on my imperfections. All of that has shifted remarkably with *Essence Repatterning*. I am finding new ways of acknowledging my strengths, moment-to-moment. This has allowed me to continually gain confidence and self-esteem, as I'm willing to notice and use the variety of talents that I *do* have.

"One way that my work has become more interesting to me is that I have been using *Essence Repatterning* with my clients. They like it and ask for 'more sessions like this.' To me, *Essence Repatterning* is not 'therapy'. It is more of an educational process, specifically, a *re-education* process. After these sessions, clients find that old limitations begin to recede and release their strangleholds. There is a lot more freedom available to them—to be vital, alive human beings.

"Finally, I'm claiming this freedom for myself, too, stretching into new areas to do things that I've told myself I could never do. I'm not so concerned now with trying to be "perfect" (which I had always used as a way of holding myself back from really participating in life). I'm now willing to take action and to be experimental. For example, I am taking private singing lessons, which is a whole different focus for me. Although I've not performed yet at the Metropolitan Opera (or even at a local club), I know I'm cookin' on many new burners, and ready to let my genuine voice be heard."

—B.A.S., physician, Chevy Chase, Md.

- "Until about five months ago, I counted myself among the many who are always looking, or hoping, to have a relationship...but who, after actively waiting for one to show up...finally found one, only to have it screw up somehow, and end, more or less, unpleasantly. I even joked about being a world-class master of being able to get over relationships and become single again. (While I do value this ability, it's not what I'd hoped to achieve.)

"Actually, *not* having a fulfilling relationship was one of the most discouraging aspects of my adult life, and one which I never seriously hoped I could turn around. However, now that has changed, and I am turning this around, in ways I could not have imagined, using *Essence Repatterning*.

"After participating in an *Essence Repatterning* seminar on relationships, I found myself attracted to a man who, like a string of others in my past, felt ambivalent toward me. During the short but rocky course of this relationship, I used *Essence Repatterning* to identify and remove an enormous load of limiting patterns that I'd grown comfortable carrying around since childhood. I already knew that *Essence Repatterning* worked for me in other areas since I'd received two unexpected promotions and a big raise since I began applying *Essence Repatterning* to my work situation. So I had the courage to look at myself honestly and remove some fairly obscure, but powerfully motivating, limiting beliefs that I'd held about myself, my family, and my prospects in life for happiness.

"Seven months have passed since that last relationship. Now I've met someone new and have been involved in what I would call a partnership/friendship for more than five months. This is a very new kind of relationship for me...we share a mutuality and willingness to work together in building a firm foundation for a future that will last. In fact, this is a goal and dream we share and actually talk about!

"This is new territory for me. Yes, there are fears and a seemingly endless number of "freshly discovered" limiting patterns to remove, and I continue to do so. At the same time, I have a newfound capacity for *receiving* love and believing in it—in ways I used to think were only available to people who were luckier than me.

"But I know it's not luck that changed things for me, because I can remember exactly how it used to be and what I did to make it happen. I am confident that this relationship is good...and now that I know what to do, I'm doing more than just hope to make sure that this relationship will last.

"To sum up my experience of *Essence Repatterning*, every couple of weeks, if not daily, I watch results I previously deemed possible only in somebody else's 'dream-come-true' show up in *my* heart, my job, my savings account and my life."

—**B.E.F., marketing director, Washington, D.C.**

See Appendix B for additional first-hand accounts of *Essence Repatterning* experiences.

2

What is
Essence Repatterning™ ?

This chapter:
1) Introduces the concept of limiting patterns;
2) Outlines Ten Success Strategies for learning the Essence Repatterning process; and
3) Gives you an opportunity to establish some benchmarks regarding where you are in your life before you begin using the process.

Essence Repatterning is a step-by-step process that allows one to:
1) Identify limiting patterns
2) Remove them and, in the process, automatically...
3) Set a new direction.

What is a Limiting Pattern?

The easiest way to identify a limiting pattern is to notice anything that you don't like in your life, or any way in which you feel stuck or immobilized. That's a limiting pattern. It's that simple.

It's not necessary to try and figure out if this "pattern" is something that has happened repeatedly. If it has happened even *once*, it is part of a bigger, overall pattern—otherwise it would not have happened at all. There would not have been a track for it. In other words, the fact that it happened, even once, is evidence that there is a track for that pattern.

A limiting pattern may be *having to commute to work longer than you want to.* It may be *having a stressful job* or *a stressful relationship.* A limiting pattern also can be *feeling blocked* or *being confused about how to move forward.*

Another way to identify limiting patterns is to notice *what you want, but don't have.* For example, if you *want* a new car and don't have one, then you have a limiting pattern of *not having a new car.* If you *want* to have your bills paid off, then you have a limiting pattern of *not having your bills paid off.* Similarly, if you *want* to be doing fulfilling work, then you have a limiting pattern of *not doing fulfilling work.*

If any of these examples fits you, or has helped you identify others that are true for you, you have begun doing the *Essence Repatterning* process. Actually, the first step, identifying the patterns, is the most challenging part of the process. However, as you remove the *top* layer of patterns—in this case, the ones you may be identifying as you read the first few chapters of this book—you will soon see the n*ext* layer of patterns to remove.

Essence Repatterning is a step-by-step process of removing one's limiting patterns, layer by layer. In this process, when you remove them, you are automatically setting a new *inner direction* toward living your life according to what *you want* today …as opposed to how you might have *thought* you had to live it, based upon the messages you received as a child.

Learning to Do *Essence Repatterning*

Although the *Essence Repatterning* process is a simple one that anyone can learn, I have found that *how* one learns it is usually the key to how well he or she uses it and how much they make it their own.

For example, I have learned that for someone to fully embrace the process—and value it enough to use it in the ways that will give that person the life-changing results desired—it is important that he or she understand the underpinnings of *why* it works, as well as *how* it works.

By learning about the nature of patterns, where they originate and why they originate, the new *re-patterner* is really learning *how* to do the process.

The secret to being a successful Essence Repatterner is in learning as much as you can about patterns, including their many varieties and permutations. As you learn how to spot patterns, and the ones from which they arise...and then the ones they give rise to, plus *others* in that neighborhood...then you will be in a good position to easily remove them, whenever and wherever you find them.

Again, *Essence Repatterning* is not a quick fix. It is a step-by-step process. If you find yourself impatient to jump right into the process, and *not* do what it takes to create the solid foundation that will make this a workable, continuing tool for you, then this book may end up on the shelf with the other self-help books you have bought but never really used.

Success Strategies

If you want to be a successful Essence Repatterner, here are some suggestions to follow:

1. **Don't believe a word I tell you...check it out.** If it works for you, work it. But *do* check it out. If you don't, you will never know if you could have made the kinds of changes that others have made using this process.
2. **Give yourself a chance to go for what you truly desire.** As you read and follow the suggested format, you may find yourself viewing your life and its possibilities differently.
3. **Start from the beginning and read each chapter in the order presented.** Each chapter builds on previous ones. In following this approach, you will be creating a solid foundation from which to take each subsequent step presented.

4. **Follow the directions suggested.** If you do, you will find that, just by reading this book, you will naturally be making some positive changes in your life.
5. **Complete the preliminary questionnaire at the end of this chapter, before you proceed any further.** (If you are reading a borrowed book, jot down the answers on a separate sheet of paper...which you can then use as a bookmark.) This is important because I have found that, many times, the changes which result from *Essence Repatterning* become so organic, one can forget how *it was*. By establishing some preliminary benchmarks, you will be giving yourself a starting place, against which to notice your progress.
6. **Claim your changes...acknowledge them to yourself.** By noticing the subtle, and obvious, changes in your life, as you are using *Essence Repatterning*, you will be encouraging this process of change by creating a feedback loop that will make future changes even easier.
7. **Decide that you are going to do this process 100 percent—and make that commitment to yourself.**
8. **Approach the material in this book freshly, as if it is brand-new and as if you have never heard of any concepts like these before.** In this way, you will not be trying to put new wine into old skins. Some of the material probably will be new, and some of it may relate to things you already know. However, you will be giving yourself the best shot at absorbing and integrating this new approach if you approach it *all* as new.
9. **Be gentle with yourself.** Go at your own pace. You will be working with patterns that have been years, and decades, in the making.
10. **Have fun.** You are embarking on a discovery process...discovering *how* you have come to be who you are presently, and discovering the changes that emerge as you *remove* those old ways of being.

If you follow these suggestions, you will be setting yourself up to *win*, not only with this new approach, but also in future learning experiences. For, as you remove just the specific limiting patterns outlined in this book, you will be making shifts in your consciousness that will allow you to use more of your innate intelligence, even brilliance, and therefore be more of who you truly are.

In the next chapter, we will begin exploring how some of our limiting patterns began and how these early experiences actually translated into *rules* for life.

Preliminary Questionnaire

Please take a few minutes to complete this questionnaire (perhaps on a separate sheet of paper, for privacy.) The purpose is to establish a *benchmark* of where you are presently as you begin using *Essence Repatterning*. This will assist you in evaluating changes as they occur. (Be as specific as seems appropriate to you.)

Note: No one else has to see this information. I suggest that you be uncompromisingly honest with yourself about current reality, where you are *right now*, in these areas. By starting with the unvarnished truth, you will be giving yourself more opportunity to change any undesirable circumstances.

Part I

1. Career/Work-Life:

2. Relationships: *(primary relationship, lovers, friends, children, parents, colleagues, etc.)*

3. Health:

4. Finances:

5. **Physical environment:** *(home/work/car)*

6. **General state of mind:** *(how life looks and feels to you...)*

7. **Other:** (issues/worries/concerns/problems not mentioned above)

8. **What do you want:** (how would you like your life to be different?)

   - If you could have it any way at all...if anything were possible, what changes would you like to make in YOUR LIFE or YOURSELF?

   - What secret strengths/abilities would you like to discover in yourself and be manifesting?

Part II

For each of the following areas, please circle the number that *generally* indicates **how satisfied** you are with that area of your life:

1. Career/Work-Life:

    least- 1 2 3 4 5 6 7 8 9 10 *-most satisfied*

2. Relationships: (primary relationship, lovers, friends, children, parents, colleagues, etc.)

    least- 1 2 3 4 5 6 7 8 9 10 *-most satisfied*

3. Health:

    least- 1 2 3 4 5 6 7 8 9 10 *-most satisfied*

4. Finances:

    least- 1 2 3 4 5 6 7 8 9 10 *-most satisfied*

5. Physical environment:

    least- 1 2 3 4 5 6 7 8 9 10 *-most satisfied*

6. General state of mind: (how life looks and feels to you...)

    least- 1 2 3 4 5 6 7 8 9 10 *-most satisfied*

7. Quality-of-Life: (Overall, how satisfied are you with your quality-of-life?)

    not very- 1 2 3 4 5 6 7 8 9 10 *-very satisfied*

8. How confident/optimistic are you about being able to have your life be the way you want it to be?

    not very- 1 2 3 4 5 6 7 8 9 10 *-very confident*

9. On-track/Off-track: (In this moment, to what degree do you feel—emotionally/mentally—that you are on-track in your life?)

    OFF-track- 1 2 3 4 5 6 7 8 9 10 *-ON-track*

3

Rules For Life

This chapter examines:
1) The concept of how and why our individual "rules for life" develop; and
2) How these rules for life affect our sense of what it means to be a man and what it means to be a woman.

When we are children, we learn how to *be*, how to navigate the world, and what to expect from the world.

Whatever we learn to *expect* is what we believe, deep down, we deserve. If we believe we deserve to be treated kindly, based upon our early experience of kind treatment, then we will assume that this is *how the world is*....you are treated kindly. Being treated kindly becomes a kind of *rule for life*....based upon our early experiences, especially those involving our high *god* and *goddess*, meaning our father and mother.

Identifying our father and mother as *god* and *goddess* may sound strange or perhaps overblown, but from a child's, even an infant's, vantage point, this is what our parents are. A child's mother is of primary importance to him or her. At the most vulnerable time of life, our mother is our sole support system, not only in terms of physical caring, but in terms of emotional nurturance as well.

Our mother's attitude toward us determines our attitude toward ourselves. If she cuddles and coos over us, we feel lovable. If she ignores our needs or keeps us at a distance, we may feel unworthy or rejected. We may conclude, based upon that perceived (or real) rejection, that we are *bad* and that something is wrong with us.

In my work with individuals, these patterns of belief and behavior show up consistently when we go underneath the conscious mind and access what is stored in the subconscious. As infants and children, we are like sponges, soaking up what the world is about, how we are supposed to be, and what to expect.

In this process, our primary models are our parents or caregivers. They teach us *who we are*, based upon how *they* regard us or how *they* treat us. They also teach us how to *be*—based upon how they treat *themselves* and how they feel about themselves.

For example, if *mom* feels like a victim (which she may have learned from her mother), chances are that we may feel like a victim too, especially if we also are female.

Mom is almighty in terms of what we believe a woman is—simply because she is our first model for womanhood. (This is true for men *and* women.) Even if she is brusque or inattentive, she is still our model for teaching us if we are lovable...or worthy of having our needs met.

Because mom is our model for womanhood—even if she actually held a strong resemblance to the proverbial wicked witch—I have found that many, if not most, of the women with whom I have worked have had a deepseated belief that...to be a woman means to be like mom.

Men, on the other hand, are naturally attracted to women who are like their mothers, since their first intimate relationship with a woman was with their mother. Consequently, for a man, that is what intimacy is about: you find a woman like mom and then recreate the kind of intimacy you had with her. Of course, many moms did not have a model for a truly nurturing relationship with a child. All they knew was what their mothers taught them.

I have found that a man will be attracted to a woman who is like his mother, no matter what, even if his mother was a shrew, self-centered, and abusive. For the son of such a mother, that is what intimacy is about: feeling left out, abused, and unappreciated.

Although we have been talking about *mom*, the same holds true for dad: he becomes our model for what a man is. Women are traditionally drawn to men like their fathers, even if it was a terrible relationship, because that is what feels natural and normal to them in terms of an intimate relationship with a man.

On the other hand, men will consciously, or subconsciously, emulate their fathers out of a belief that that is what it means to be a man.

Being a Man

It is often startling to see the lengths a man will go to be like his father. In my work with Al, a man in his 30s, I found that even though he hated his dad for his abusiveness, especially toward Al's mother, Al himself also was very abusive and prone to violence. But this was a side of himself that he hated and judged. At the same time, there were obvious other aspects to Al that were peace-loving and spiritually-seeking.

Despite these gentle parts of himself, Al found himself naturally drawn to situations in which he would be volatile and violent. Although he was not a bully, as his father was, he was quick to perceive injustice in school and elsewhere and begin violently acting like a vigilante, bringing his own style of justice.

When we discovered that these patterns were arising out of a belief that to be a man meant to be like his father, he confided that he was afraid to date women because he didn't want to be abusive. Unconsciously knowing his tendencies toward his father's style of behavior, his deep moral code kept him out of intimate situations with women, situations in which he might act like his father. It was as if being violent with men was as far as he would go in terms of being a man. Since he believed that being a man (hence, being like his father) meant abusing the woman in his life, then he just wouldn't have a woman in his life.

It is interesting to note that, even though Al believed he *had* to be violent and abusive, as his father was, he found a way to act this out in situations that could fit his moral code. In other words, he had created an outlet for these patterns that he could somehow rationalize to himself.

These deeply imbedded beliefs about what it means to be a man or a woman can be so tenacious, in fact, that we will unknowingly act, on a daily basis, in the very ways we may have despised our mother or father for acting.

Being a Woman

One example of this is Margo, an attractive, self-directed mother of two in her 30s, who was afraid that she would raise her daughters the way her mother had raised her and her siblings. As soon as she voiced her fear, my antenna went up because I have found that *whatever we fear arises out of a belief that that is how things are supposed to be.* In other words, the only reason we will fear something happening is because it is what, on a deep, subconscious level, we think *should* happen. Another way of saying this is that our fears reflect what we believe are the *rules for life*.

When I asked Margo how her mother had raised her, she said resentfully: "Repressed, dependent, and compliant." When I tested Margo's body, through Applied Kinesiology (or muscle-testing; see Appendix A), and asked if she had a limiting pattern of raising her children to be repressed, dependent and compliant, the answer was a clear *yes*.

Needless to say, Margo was shocked at her body's clear response. As the session progressed and the full truth of that pattern unfolded, Margo was devastated to realize that, in some very telling ways, she had been raising her children just as her mother had raised her, the very thing she had vowed she would never do. When we discovered that she believed her mother was the *model* for being a woman and a mother, it all made sense.

> Soon after that session, Margo noticed changes in herself and in her treatment of her daughters. Since then, she has learned to do E*ssence Repatterning* on her own and has been repatterning other behaviors and attitudes that have blocked her from expressing her true Self and from having the harmonious family life she desires.

One way to know what our *rules for life* are is to listen to what we say to ourselves. As I worked with Sylvia, a divorced mother of five in her 40s, she complained about "doing all the wrong things," specifically being overweight and smoking, both of which were contrary to her particular religious mores. As we talked, she realized that she was often saying to herself such things as "Oh, you're going to do it wrong"....or "You're going to trust the wrong people; you always do."

We discovered that Sylvia was living out a meta-pattern, an all-pervasive pattern, of *feeling wrong*. This meant that, deep down inside, she subconsciously *believed that she was wrong* and, in fact, that she *should feel wrong*....that it was a *rule for life*. As a *rule for life*, she believed that it was the *natural order of things* for her to feel as if she was wrong.

Since that was her belief, based upon her upbringing, that is what she told herself was the required, necessary way to be. Consequently, her self-talk reflected that, as did her actions.

Another common form of self-talk I have found is that of telling ourselves: "I can't do it"..."I don't have what it takes."... "If I try this, I'll fail"..."I'm no good; I'm worthless."

Based on studies in which researchers followed two-year-olds around and tallied how many times they were given negative messages, or told "No" in a day, compared to "Yes," they found the ratio was 435 no's to 30 yes's, a ratio of 14 to 1. When you add this to the number of times a child is told "You're a bad boy/girl," it shouldn't be too surprising to learn how deeply imbedded this negative self-talk is.

Our self-talk often keeps us in a tyranny of fear as well. Although these may sound like strong words, I have found that much of our self-talk arises out of deep-seated fears, and therefore beliefs, that we are bad, flawed, broken, and irreparably damaged. Most people with whom I have worked have their own version of these words, some of which are considerably more brutal than these examples.

If this sounds extreme, bear in mind that my work and research have been with healthy individuals who are naturally drawn to opportunities to grow, change and learn what is holding them back from having the kind of life they consciously desire. Many of them are successful in their fields. Many, if not most, have done significant amounts of personal-growth work and have a spiritual focus. Many of them meditate. Basically, they are generally as well-adjusted as one can be while living out the limiting patterns that seem to be a natural part of the human condition. The point is that, with every client with whom I have worked, some form of these deep-seated negative beliefs has consistently surfaced to be identified and removed.

I personally don't find it disturbing to discover yet another self-sabotaging belief, or fear, within myself. On the contrary, I am grateful. By knowing about it, I can remove it. If I don't know about it, or am afraid to own it, then I'm stuck with it and the self-sabotage that goes with it.

The good news about limiting patterns is that *whatever we can identify, we can remove.* It's important to remember this. It is no longer necessary to drag them around or, more accurately, let them lead us around by the nose.

Occasionally in a seminar individuals will express discomfort or fear at identifying their negative aspects. They say they are afraid that talking about them will give them more power. They have learned to "think positively" as the cure for those aspects. Unfortunately, that just glosses over the truth, and we are still stuck with the limiting patterns.

With *Essence Repatterning,* you can identify the pattern and *remove* it. It also allows you to identify many patterns at one time and remove them simultaneously.

If you are feeling somewhat threatened about the possibility of discovering some uncomfortable limiting patterns in yourself, that is not unusual. We each have aspects of ourselves that are *invested* in maintaining the status quo. These old aspects of ourselves are most comfortable with what is familiar, whether it be pain, fear, or even abuse (including self-abuse).

It is useful to know that in *Essence Repatterning,* whatever patterns are identified and removed are those we are specifically ready to release. The changes that result are those we can easily integrate. If we are not ready to remove a particular pattern, we may not even notice its existence.

If you see a limiting pattern and don't want to remove it, you won't. For example, perhaps you stopped smoking cigarettes at some point in your life. Chances are, it was when you decided to. That is how *Essence Repatterning* works as well. When you want to remove a limiting pattern, you can.

The process is simple. The next few chapters will teach you how to do that and, just as important, help you learn to *identify* the patterns themselves. That is where the challenge lies.

Note: In the Introduction, I suggested that, to get the most out of the time you invest in reading this book, you jot down any limiting patterns that occur to you as you are learning the *Essence Repatterning* process. That way you will be identifying your first batch of limiting patterns and be ready to remove them when you reach that part of the process. By the way, as you are listing your patterns, the best words to use are exactly those that come to mind, or that describe any experiences you may remember.

4

Limiting Patterns

In this chapter you will learn:
1) How to do the step-by-step Essence Repatterning process; and
2) Why it is important to include in the removal process all the various permutations for each limiting pattern being addressed.

What *are* limiting patterns? How can we identify them?

Limiting patterns are all around us. They are as close as our biggest—and smallest—complaints about life.

What are some of the things that annoy, or irritate, you the most right now? Perhaps it's having a cranky boss or being overweight.

If so, you have limiting patterns of:

> *Pattern: Having a cranky boss*
> *Pattern: Being overweight*

Now, think of something you want but don't have. Let's say it's a new car, or perhaps a fulfilling relationship.

These unfulfilled desires represent limiting patterns as well, the patterns of:

> *P:* **Not** *having a new car*
> *P:* **Not** *having a fulfilling relationship.*

> **DEFINITION OF A LIMITING PATTERN:**
> 1. Something you **have** in your life that you don't *want*.
> 2. Something you **want** but don't *have*.

Where to Start

If limiting patterns are all around you, you may be wondering where to begin. The simplest approach I have found is: Start where you are.

In other words, what are you feeling right now? To create a starting place, let's say you have had a stressful day and that, for one reason or another, you feel anxious...even scared...and possibly overwhelmed. (You don't have to understand *why* the feelings are there. As you proceed with this process, you will gain more awareness of what gives rise to particular limiting patterns. However, it is not necessary to know that in order to begin.)

By noticing these particular feelings, you will have identified three limiting patterns: those of *feeling anxious, scared,* and *overwhelmed*.

One way to begin working with the *Essence Repatterning* process *in the moment* is to write them down as limiting patterns:

    P: Feeling anxious
    P: Feeling scared
    P: Feeling overwhelmed

To repattern these *specific* limiting patterns of *feeling anxious, scared* and *overwhelmed,* simply use your conscious mind to direct your unconscious by saying:

> **I choose to reframe these patterns, and all allied limiting patterns, now—and to know it.**

> *Note: I will say more about this choice later in the chapter. The material covered here will provide a context for that explanation.*

Now that you've done that, you *may* feel easier. You will have removed the patterns of *feeling anxious, scared, and overwhelmed* in the moment.

However, perhaps you also have limiting patterns of be*ing anxious*, *being scared*, and *being overwhelmed*. These are completely separate patterns that may *seem* like the same experience as *feeling anxious, scared,* and *overwhelmed*—but they are not.

Beach Ball Metaphor

The metaphor I use to explain this is that of a very large, multi-colored beach ball that is made up of many, many panels. Each panel represents one limiting pattern.

As we look at limiting patterns, it helps to think of each *subject area* we're addressing as a *separate beach ball* comprised of many panels, or limiting patterns. If you had this big beach ball in front of you right now, you probably would notice that some of these limiting patterns stand out more than others. Those are the ones that are ripe for identifying and removing. As we identify each one, we are putting it *on-line* or, in other words, flagging it to be removed later.

Once we have identified and put *on-line* all of the patterns that seem appropriate in one sitting, then we will remove the whole batch of them at once, that is, everything that has been put *on-line* to that point.

In the beach-ball metaphor, when we remove those patterns, or panels, it is as if we are actually *collapsing* the identified panels/patterns. Then the beach ball will be smaller, and you may see other limiting patterns that you hadn't noticed before. Because you have removed the most obvious patterns, it will be easier to see some of the more subtle ones, or what I call the next layer.

In the example with which we have begun, the beach ball we're examining is that of *negative feelings/experiences in the moment*.

Although you have removed—or collapsed—the panels on

the beach ball that represent *feeling* anxious, scared, and *overwhelmed*, there may be other panels that represent *being anxious, scared,* and *overwhelmed.*

There may be still others that represent *thinking* in ways that are *anxious, scary,* and *overwhelming.*

There also may be others that represent *acting* anxious, scared, and *overwhelmed.*

Notice that any of these could register generally as *being anxious, scared,* and *overwhelmed.*

The key is to remove as many aspects as possible of whichever limiting pattern you are addressing.

I have found that, for each specific pattern, there are more than 40 versions of that one pattern that must be removed in order to deal with it inclusively. This chapter will discuss those permutations and then teach you how to work with them easily and efficiently. (**Note:** It is unnecessary to remember each of these permutations. However, it is important have a general understanding of the overall framework which they comprise.)

Identifying the Permutations

Let's use the issue of *being anxious* as an example. If we are to fully remove a particular pattern, I have found that some of the permutations we need to include are:

Pattern: **Being** anxious
P: **Believing** that you are anxious
P: **Feeling** anxious
P: **Thinking** anxiously
P: **Actin**g anxiously
P: **Assuming** that you are anxious
P: **Perceiving** that you are anxious
P: **Considering** that you are anxious

I also have discovered that even if all of these patterns are removed, there still may be some experience of anxiety because you may be *telling yourself that this* (*being* or *feeling anxious*) *is how it has to be…how it must be…*and *that it's what you deserve.*

Even then, although you have removed all of the above patterns, there may still be some form of anxiety because you may be telling yourself and/or believing that you **should** *feel, be, think, act, assume, perceive,* and *consider* that you are anxious.

This also applies to telling yourself and/or believing that you **ought** to *feel, be, think, act, assume, perceive,* and *consider* that you are anxious.

Other related patterns include telling yourself and/or believing that you **must...have to...that it's required...demanded ...essential... necessary...expected...** that you *feel, be, think, act, assume, perceive,* and *consider* that you are anxious.

Another aspect to this particular beach ball may be telling yourself and/or believing that if you **don't** *feel, be, think, act, assume, perceive, consider* this way, you *will be punished* (often severely). For most deeply imbedded patterns, I have found that the consequences individuals fear usually include believing that they will die, or perhaps cease to exist.

When an individual believes his/her survival is at stake, it means that they have incorporated, and are holding, these particular patterns as ***rules for life.***

Rules For Life

One way to understand the concept of *rules for life* is to imagine that, when you were a child, no matter how old you were, or where your family lived, the interior walls of your home were always painted bright blue. Just now, imagine that when you were a child, that is all you ever saw: bright blue walls. Day in, and day out. Bright blue walls.

In fact, since that was the only experience you had to draw from in a daily, consistent fashion, as far as you knew, that was how life was. You had bright blue walls. After all, that is the color of the walls your parents chose, and provided. It must be right. What other reference did you have on such a continual basis?

So imagine now that you have grown up and are out on your own, selecting your first apartment or living situation.

> Guess what color walls you are going to have? If it isn't bright blue, you can be sure it will be something close to it, even if it's just in the closet, out of sight. (Of course, someone may say, "Well, I am *not* going to have bright blue walls in *my* home I am my own person. I have set my own direction. *My* walls are...azure blue." Right, and notice that they are still blue. Or perhaps you *don't* see any blue walls in your home, but...if you peel back the wallpaper, guess what you will find...right. Blue walls. That early programming can be tenacious.)
>
> Now substitute for the *blue walls*, the experience of *feeling anxious*, or *feeling as if you are walking on eggshells*. If what you grew up with was an atmosphere of tension, anxiety, and fear or tentativeness, that's the color you will paint the walls of your life experience. Those patterns will have become some of your *rules for life*.

As long as I have worked with this concept, I am still amazed to see how consistently it plays out. Although it is always risky to make a generalization, it does appear that anything that we're experiencing negatively in our lives probably reflects some patterns, or versions of patterns, that we saw or experienced as children. This is perhaps seen most easily in the areas of self-esteem.

For example, if we are feeling a lack of confidence or unworthiness in a personal relationship, it is highly unlikely that this is an isolated incident. If we are truthful, we will usually discover that we have experienced those feelings other times, perhaps many times, through the years. In fact, we may find that that the way we are feeling in that particular relationship reflects a painful way we felt in an early relationship with one or both of our parents or parent-figures.

Although this might bring up some poignant memories, remember, these are all j*ust* limiting patterns...and what we can identify as a limiting pattern, we can remove.

The Natural Order of Things

When I first discovered the concept of *rules for life*, it was as a result of uncovering beliefs about what I call *the natural order of things*. This refers to those limiting attitudes and convictions that fall into the category of, "Well, that's just how life is."

This led me to identifying additional permutations for a given pattern, including patterns of believing that:

"This is how it is...always has been....and always will be, and there's nothing I can do about it...It's hopeless, will never change, and I am doomed to it being this way...I have no choice in the matter and I'm helpless to change it. ...I'm a victim of circumstances."

Positive Thinkers

These patterns may sound, or feel, rather negative to you. It's about this time that some individuals start getting squeamish and saying, "This feels bad. I don't like to focus on the negative. I only want to focus on the positive."

Perhaps, as mentioned in the last chapter, they fear that discussing these patterns gives the patterns more weight and more power over them. Others may start feeling as if they are spiraling downward into that hopeless feeling described above.

Judy, an urban planner in one of the early *Essence Repatterning* seminars, wrestled with these concerns initially. As with many of us, myself included, she had learned to be a *positive* thinker. In fact, some of her personal-growth work had taught her to avoid any unpleasant thoughts and to say *"cancel, cancel"* to anything she feared might be negative programming.

As limiting patterns were identified during the seminar, Judy says that she busily tried to negate them, reprogram them and, she sees now, generally cling to something that had worked *for* her in the past in ways that *limited* her present growth opportunity.

Although she was scared of what the *positive-thinker* part of her said about the process of naming the truth of these limiting patterns, she says she kept returning to the class because of the exciting changes other participants were reporting in their lives.

Now a trained *Essence Repatterning* practitioner herself, Judy welcomes the truth, using any limiting patterns it reveals to move herself forward, rather than to keep herself feeling scared and helpless. She sees now that her initial fear was a tool her ego tried to use to sabotage her growth and movement out of the old, familiar patterns. Today she is applying her talents in an area that has long been a dream—assisting individuals and community groups to resolve conflict and to work more effectively, using *Essence Repatterning* as one of her tools.

Judy demonstrated to herself, as many others have, that although it initially might feel uncomfortable to identify the limiting patterns, to bring them up, and put them *on-line* as it were—the payoff is that once they are repatterned, you will no longer be stuck with these particular patterns.

The truth is that these limiting patterns have been stuck in our craw, buried in our subconscious for a long time, quietly eating away at our peace of mind, undermining our sense of self and sabotaging our feelings of well-being. What we are doing when we shine the light on them is identifying them for what they are—limiting ways of seeing, feeling, and experiencing our lives.

This is not giving them *more* power. It is giving them less. We are finally seeing them as *limiting patterns*, rather than "the way life is," and "the way life has to be."

It may be that when we retreat into *positive* thinking, rather than *reality* thinking—acknowledging *what is* rather than what we'd like to *think* it is, we do so because the truth of reality is so painful. However, with *Essence Repatterning*, once you have identified the truth of the limiting pattern, you are not stuck with it. You can reframe that pattern...and, in effect, change your reality.

Camouflaged Patterns

Some of these limiting beliefs are so deeply buried and camouflaged that you may not relate to them emotionally or mentally. The good news is that you can remove them anyway.

If there is any possibility that some aspect of a limiting pattern mentioned here might be stored in your subconscious and, therefore, might be holding you back—even the tiniest bit—it is to your advantage to remove that particular pattern when we come to that part of the process. If you don't, and if you only remove the obvious ones, you are leaving the ego something to dredge up later to help you feel as limited as you always have and thereby maintain the status quo.

Limiting Ego

If we want to change our limiting patterns and behaviors, it helps to understand the *limiting ego*. When we are very young, it is our ego that helps keep us alive. That is its job: to keep us alive. So whatever it perceives to be necessary to accomplish that, it is going to follow. This includes following any perceived *rule for life*.

Today, as adults, the ego is still doing its job. If you step out into oncoming traffic, it is your ego that tells you to "Jump back," out of danger. If you have skipped a meal and your body needs sustenance, it is your ego that reminds you it is time to eat.

However, if you find yourself over-indulging in things that aren't healthy for you, that is your limit*ing ego* at work, urging you to do those things that will bring you down, or keep you *feeling small* and *insecure,* and living according to your *rules for life.*

Letting the *limiting ego* run the show is what has kept each of us, to some extent anyway, feeling disempowered and out of control. The way to take back our power is to re-educate the ego, re-pattern the old *rules for life*, and give ourselves specific new directions for how we want to be living our lives now, as consciously choosing adults. This is what *Essence Repatterning* is about.

Who's Driving *Your* Horse-drawn Carriage?

To understand the *limiting ego*, imagine one of those old-time, black silhouette pictures of a horse-drawn, covered carriage. In this metaphor, the driver who is sitting up on the board, holding the reins and directing the horses is the *limiting ego*. He has been in charge so long that he has even forgotten that there is a carriage behind him, or that *you* are in that carriage. Furthermore, he has forgotten that *you* are actually his employer—that *you* have the right to call the shots and direct this carriage, i.e., your life.

Now think of how many years you have been riding around in that carriage. How old are you? That is how long the ego has been running the show, according to the same rules, year in and year out. Until we catch on and start changing these patterns, much of the time our ego sits up there telling us what to do and when to do it, without us even realizing what's going on.

If you are reading this book, you probably have been doing some self-help and personal-growth work, perhaps a lot of it. I would imagine that much, if not all, that you have done up until now probably has been aimed, in one way or another, at taking back the reins from your *limiting ego*. With *Essence Repatterning* you can learn to do this with specific patterns in a very lasered way.

In the last chapter I alluded to the ego's attachment to the status quo and to staying in control. Some of the ways it tries to do this are by keeping us small, dragging its heels, and actually fighting against anything that will allow you, yourSelf, to be your own master rather than letting the ego be your master.

This is not to make the ego wrong. It definitely has its place. It *is* in charge of your survival. However, what you are learning to do with this process is *change* the rules for survival.

In fact, what if you were to stop congratulating yourself for being a *survivor*, as so many people do—and open up to the possibility of *thriving*, in the best sense of the word?

That is what is possible with *Essence Repatterning*.

More Permutations

Just as there can be patterns of believing that certain ways of thinking and behaving are *the natural order of things* and therefore essential to our survival, there are corollary beliefs that if we did **not** think or behave that way, we would not exist....because such treatment or behavior would be **out of** *the natural order of things*. This puts us in the position of believing we *need* the limiting pattern in order to exist.

> One example of this was demonstrated by my client, Marilyn, a swinging single, vibrant redhead in her early 60s, who looks much younger. The first time we worked together, she put her arms up to be muscle-tested, and brightly said: "Ask me if I'm an alcoholic."
>
> Surprised, I said, "Why do you want me to ask that?"
>
> "Well, I always have a glass of wine poured throughout the day, but I don't really drink much of it."
>
> When I asked, through muscle-testing, "Is there a limiting pattern of Marilyn being an alcoholic?" The answer was clearly *no*. Then I asked, "Does Marilyn believe she *should* be an alcoholic?" That answer was *yes*.
>
> Surprised, I asked her to explain. "Well, my parents were alcoholics and my brothers and sisters all are," she said. As we checked further through muscle-testing, it became clear that Marilyn believed it was a *rule for life* to be an alcoholic and that she was at least trying to play by the rules by thinking or suspecting she was, or at least trying to act as if she was.

Minimum Daily Requirements

In addition to our *rules for life*, I have found that, within these *rules*, there may also be *minimum daily requirements*, or *daily needs*, for some limiting patterns. The basic difference between a *rule for life* and a *daily need* is that of intensity.

For example, suppose Mary has a pattern of *believing she has to feel anxious,* as a *rule for life*. With that pattern, she will have a specific tolerance for how much or how often she has to feel anxious. Perhaps she just needs to feel it three or four days a month. In that case, if she has a good week or two, without anxiety, she might start feeling "as if the other shoe is going to drop," actually anticipating something bad happening. (Of course, this, in itself, is enough to provoke a dose of anxiety.) If yet another stress-free week goes by, inevitably something will happen to help her stay within her anxiety "tolerances."

But what if she had a *daily need* for anxiety—as many people do? Then she will have what I call a "minimum daily requirement" for anxiety. Once again, it doesn't have to be played out every minute of the day, just enough to fulfill the beliefs about "how life is."

To demonstrate the principle of a *daily need* in a seminar, I asked participants to think of an unpleasant aspect of their life that they experienced every day. Immediately, Janice, a dramatic woman in the back of the room, an association executive in her 50s, began urgently waving her arm to be recognized. When called on, she said that her issue was that she commuted to and from work three to four hours each day by public transportation.

Although I had hoped to elicit a more universal example of a daily need, I asked her to come up to the front of the room. As I began muscle-testing her to determine what limiting patterns this unpleasant daily commute fulfilled, we found that, indeed, it did represent a rather common daily need—the daily need *to experience life as struggle*.

Although Janice used the commute to fulfill that need five

days a week, she found other ways to struggle on the weekend...keeping herself on edge...feeling as if there was never enough time to do all the things she had to do...etc.

Since she has removed these particular patterns, Janice has learned to drive, interviewed for other jobs more conveniently located, and begun considering moving her residence to a more desirable location. She also is making her commuting time work for her by using that time to identify and remove limiting patterns each day.

Perhaps you are noticing one of your *daily needs*. I have found that many people have *minimum daily requirements* for feeling pain, humiliation, shame, punished, wrong, out-of-balance, separate, isolated, disconnected, unsafe, and abandoned...to name just a few. The good news is that now we can remove these patterns. They no longer need to control us.

If You Want to Be Alive...

When we include the patterns related to survival issues (believing that *it has to be this way in order for us to survive, or exist*), then usually there are corollary patterns of believing that *if it isn't* this way, then we *won't* exist.

One example of this is the pattern of *believing* that being anxious is a *rule for life*. If we believe that we have to be anxious in order to be alive, or exist, we will probably find the corollary belief that **not** being anxious is *inconsistent* with the *rules*.

Another way of saying this is that there is probably a belief that anything that keeps us from feeling anxious, at least to some extent... is *against the rules*. Taking this the next step, this would mean that feeling calm and peaceful would be *against the rules*—if we want to exist.

Needless to say, survival is a powerful motivator. If we believe that a behavior is tied to our survival, that we **need** it to survive, we will be tenacious in clinging to that pattern of behavior, even if it means pain, humiliation, and suffering.

What Is One of Your *Rules*?

You can demonstrate that for yourself right now. What is one *unpleasant* behavior, pattern, *way of being*, or aspect of life that you *know*, or tell yourself, is necessary to your survival—even though it may not make any sense to your mind?

Some of the answers that I have heard to that question include: *not making too much money...not being too fulfilled...not being too happy...not being too successful...*or *too smart...*or *being seen too much...*or *too big for my britches.*

Where do these answers come from? They are based upon our conclusions about what the *rules for life* are, based upon what we experienced and observed while growing up.

Our life force is so powerful that if we believe, for example, that it's a *rule for life* to *feel anxious*, then we actually will be *invested* in feeling anxious. We will *want* to be anxious because, in this belief system, our life depends upon it. We also will probably have patterns of being *attached* to feeling anxious, *obsessed* with it, even *addicted* to it. We also will, to one degree or another, *resist* it being any other way, and actually *hold any other way at bay*.

This is how much we want to survive. Since virtually all of our limiting patterns arise out of our perceived *rules for life*, then **what motivates these limiting patterns of behavior is the desire to live,** rather than die. It is important to remember this. These behaviors were adopted originally to help us, not limit us. These were the coping strategies our ego learned to help us survive.

Moving Forward

Of course we have all changed through the years, growing, expanding, often moving forward, sometimes moving backwards, or sideways, but usually moving. Where does the ego fit into all of this expansion and movement?

What I have seen in case after case is that no matter what

progress we make—and we do make tremendous progress, sometimes against seemingly impossible odds—to one degree or another, it still is played out, and limited by, those original *rules for life*. This is why it is essential to address those *rules*.

Why can't we just tell the *limiting ego* to cut it out, back off, or take a vacation? Unfortunately, that doesn't do the trick. As mentioned, it is tenacious and wily. It has been in charge so long that it believes *its* survival and identity are at stake if we attempt to make any major changes in our life or the *rules* we live by.

Even when we begin changing the limiting patterns that have brought us *pain*, the ego feels threatened and fearful for its existence. Therefore, it is important to realize there may also be limiting patterns of the *limiting ego* using *feeling anxious* (or whatever limiting patterns we're identifying) as a way to *control and manipulate us*, while simultaneously keeping itself in charge. Additional permutations include our *allowing* the *limiting ego* to do this, *listening to it, believing it,* and *being and feeling victimized by it.*

Meta-Patterns

Finally, the last permutation we should include to remove, in case it is in there, is that of the *meta-pattern*.

A meta-pattern is an all-encompassing limiting pattern that pervades our whole life. If someone had a meta-pattern of *feeling anxious*, for example, it would mean that he would experience life as if he was wearing glasses with lenses that filtered everything he saw through the meta-pattern of *feeling anxious... having to feel anxious...believing he should feel anxious... must feel anxious...* etc. Another way of looking at it is that it would be as if he were living in a dream, or a cloud of *having to feel anxious* so that every experience was filtered through that limiting pattern.

For example, if he went to buy a new suit, he would view the options through that pattern. (He might feel anxious about making the right choice, or anxious about how fat or thin he appears in a suit he is trying on.) If he received a compliment, he would hear it through that pattern. (If someone told him he had done a good job on a particular task, he might hear it as a negative comment on the quality of previous tasks he had performed but which were not mentioned. He also might feel anxious about having to measure up to that compliment in the future.) If he were interviewing for a new job, or just reading the classified ads, he would do it through the limiting pattern of having *to feel anxious*. (He might feel anxious about how he is presenting himself in an interview, or he might filter potential job opportunities through anxious self-criticism that "I really couldn't handle that job.")

By including *meta-patterns* in the list of possible permutations to be removed for each limiting pattern, I am not suggesting that one would necessarily remove *all* of the ways in which this meta-pattern might play out. There is a specific process for doing this which is more suitably taught in a seminar setting. (There is also an audio tape available—listed in the back of the book—which allows the listener to remove more detailed aspects of specific meta-patterns.)

However, by including the category of *meta-patterns* in this *umbrella* of permutations, if there are any meta-patterns present in the limiting patterns you are reframing, it *is* possible to remove *some* aspects of them...as always, it will be only those aspects that you are ready to remove and whose resulting changes you can easily integrate.

Subconscious and Unconscious

The limiting patterns we have been discussing and putting on-line are stored in what is called, for the purposes of this process, the *subconscious*. Think of it as a warehouse, with shelf after shelf of patterns, neatly categorized, from which the ego picks whatever it believes it needs to do its job of keeping us alive.

In a moment, as you did earlier in this chapter, you are going to be working with another part of your being which, for these purposes, is called the *unconscious*. In this process, the *unconscious* is the reservoir of your highest potential. Everything that is possible for you (probably far more than your ego might think) is available there. You may use other words to describe it. For example, in working with *Essence Repatterning*, some people think of the *unconscious* as another way of saying *Spirit, God*, or simply the *All*. However, the process works whether or not one has a clear conscious definition of what this means to them.

What we have been doing in this chapter is setting up an all-encompassing approach to removing a wide variety of permutations for each limiting pattern to be addressed. These permutations have been incorporated into a simple, easy-to-follow format that is spelled out later in this chapter. Now you will have an opportunity to begin experimenting with it—using the three limiting patterns with which we began, plus any others you have identified and written down

Pattern: Feeling anxious
P: Feeling scared
P: Feeling overwhelmed

Basic Essence Repatterning Format

A. ***Write down*** all of the limiting patterns you want to remove:
   1. Any patterns you have identified as you read this chapter and previous ones;
   2. The three patterns listed above (even if you are not feeling these patterns now, most people experience *anxiety, overwhelm,* or *being scared* at one time or another, so it's a safe bet that they are candidates for removal).

B. The next step is to ***include all of the various permutations*** for each of these patterns—to ensure that you don't leave any aspect of these specific patterns in place to manifest at a later time.

- To do this, turn to page 46-47 and read all of the permutations listed under **No. 1**, beginning with the words: **"For each of these patterns, I'm including all of the associated limiting patterns of:"**

C. *Remove* all of these limiting patterns...by consciously directing the unconscious to *reframe* these patterns.

Note: When we direct the unconscious to reframe these patterns, we are asking it to *generate and begin utilizing new behaviors that are superior to these* (limiting patterns) *for providing the intended benefit.*

1. Remember, the intended benefit of these limiting patterns has been survival. As explained in this chapter, limiting patterns originate out of a belief that *this is how life is...this is the natural order of things...these are the rules for life;* in other words, *that this is what it takes for us to survive, to be alive.*
2. It may serve you, as you are doing this process, to remember that every limiting pattern arises out of a *pure* intention—an intention to keep us alive. This is based upon what we learned, or experienced as children, were the *rules for life.*
3. As we direct the unconscious to *reframe* these patterns, we're asking it to create new patterns—new patterns of thought, feeling, and behavior—that are superior to the old limiting patterns to provide the intended benefit of staying alive. In effect, we are directing the unconscious to **rewrite** the *rules* for our life—in ways that are more aligned with our essence and who we are today. Remember, up until now, most of us have been living according to *rules* that were installed decades ago, when we were very young. These *rules* may have served to keep us alive then, but they are outdated now.

4. To reframe these patterns, do so by making the choice written under **No. 2** on page 47, beginning with the words:
   "I choose to reframe these patterns..."

D. Take a moment to *receive the inner changes* you have created.

Note: When you **choose to reframe** the limiting patterns you have listed, you are *automatically* setting a new direction within you. It is not necessary to do any more than this. However, as you continue reading this book, later you will learn how to work consciously with this new direction in specific ways if you so desire.

Once you have completed your first *Essence Repatterning*, here is a short form you can use in the future:

Basic *Essence Repatterning*

A. *Write down* all of the limiting patterns you want to remove/reframe.

B. *Include all the permutations* for each of these patterns by reading the permutations listed on next page under **No. 1**, beginning with the words:
   "For each of these patterns, I'm including all of the associated limiting patterns of:"

C. *Remove/Reframe* all of these limiting patterns by making the choice written under **No. 2** on page 47, beginning with the words:
   "I choose to reframe these patterns..."

D. Take a moment to *receive the inner changes* you have created.

E. When you are ready, return to A, above, and begin identifying the next layer of patterns you want to remove.

Essence Repatterning

1. **Identify Limiting Pattern(s)**—*After having written down **all** of the* Limiting Patterns you want to reframe at this time, say to yourself:

   "For each of these patterns, I'm including all of the associated limiting patterns of:

   ➡ Being this way...and believing, feeling, thinking, acting, assuming, perceiving, considering...that it's true...

   ➡ Telling myself this is how it has to be, must be, and what I deserve...

   ➡ That it should be this way, ought to be, must be, has to be, is required, essential, necessary, demanded, expected, wrong if I don't, punished (or worse) if I don't...

   ➡ That this is how it is, always has been, always will be...
   - There's nothing I can do about it...
   - It will never change...
   - I have no choice...I'm powerless...
   - It's hopeless...

   ➡ That it's the Natural order of things *(Rule for life...)*

   ➡ That it's a *DAILY Need* (In case there's a Minimum Daily Requirement)

   —*continue on next page*

➡ That my survival is at stake...(Believing that if I want to be alive, this is how it/I have to be...) Therefore, I'm including being:

- Attached to it being this way...
- Invested in it being this way...
- Wanting it to be this way...
- Being obsessed...Addicted to it being this way...
- Resistant to it being any other way...
- Holding any other way at bay...

➡ I'm including any *'Limiting ego'* involvement, such as:
- Being controlled by *'limiting ego'*... Manipulated by it...
- Allowing it, listening to it, believing it...
- Being and feeling victimized by it...

➡ I'm including any Meta-pattern...in case this is an all-encompassing pattern that pervades my whole life.

2. <u>**Reframe** all of the above Limiting Patterns at one time...</u>

To do this, say:

"I choose to reframe these patterns and all allied limiting patterns now—and to know it."

Congratulations, you have just reframed your first batch of limiting patterns. To help you identify the next layer of patterns that may emerge, let's look at what you have done as a result of removing the patterns we used as examples:

> P: *Feeling anxious*
> P: *Feeling scared*
> P: *Feeling overwhelmed*

If you followed the Basic *Essence Repatterning* process just outlined and removed these patterns, and *all* of their permutations—by reading and including them—these patterns are gone, they have all been reframed, at least in the *specific way they were worded.*

You have collapsed these particular patterns on the beach ball we discussed earlier. Because these most obvious patterns are gone, now you may see others that you hadn't noticed before.

The patterns you begin noticing now will fall into one of two general categories: horizontal patterns or vertical patterns.

Horizontal Patterns

Horizontal patterns are those that may look like and feel like one another, but which aren't precisely the same and, in fact, have different words to describe them. Remember, **the subconscious is very literal and precise in how it stores our limiting patterns.** So we need to be as precise as we can in identifying the patterns we want to remove.

For example, if we are talking about *feeling anxious,* other horizontal patterns it would be useful to consider are those such as: *feeling **nervous, stressed out, uptight, jittery,*** etc.

It's important to understand the concept of horizontal patterns because, if you have removed *feeling **anxious*** and all of its permutations, later you may feel something that could be *masquerading* as anxiety. What you would be feeling would be a horizontal pattern that you have *not* removed and that the *lim-*

iting ego has drawn from its remaining stock of limiting patterns to try to keep you feeling the same old familiar way.

Every time you do E*ssence Repatterning,* you are reducing the limiting ego's inventory of limiting patterns. The most efficient way I have found to do this process is, for every single limiting pattern I notice, to also identify as many horizontal ones like it as I can think of. We just did that, above, with *feeling anxious.* What would some horizontal patterns be for *feeling scared?*

You could include: *feeling fearful...afraid...threatened... unsafe...ambushed...terrorized...terror-stricken...at risk... under the gun...alone... isolated...*and on and on.

Everyone will have specific words that register for them. However, I have found that most of the examples cited in this book are commonly held limiting patterns—even if you are not conscious of the pattern at the moment. For that reason, if you are in doubt about whether or not a particular limiting pattern is yours, I suggest that you include it to be reframed. Why not? **You will never add a limiting pattern by doing so, and you might remove one that is sabotaging you or creating a blockage for you.**

There is an additional benefit in identifying—and removing—as many horizontal patterns as you can at any one time. As you remove more and more horizontal patterns it will be easier to see some of the vertical patterns which are associated with the horizontal ones.

Vertical Patterns

Vertical patterns are those patterns that exist:

1) **Above** the pattern you are addressing—these may be patterns that arise from the pattern you're considering. (For example, feel*ing anxious,* may give rise to the pattern of *feeling uncomfortable* in groups of people...or *feeling afraid to drive in traffic.)*

2) **Below** the pattern you are addressing. (In this case *feeling anxious,* may be one manifestation of a more fundamental

pattern of *believing that you're not good enough*...or *believing that you are bad)*.

Before we move on, I want to offer you a reminder that we have all spent many years playing out our limiting patterns, and that there are usually many layers and configurations of them. As this work unfolded and developed, I often would assume I had handled something...completely washed it out of my life...only to find that what I had handled was *that* particular phase or level of it.

For example, when I realized that *shame* was a limiting pattern of mine, I initially thought that if I repatterned *shame*, then I would be done with it and never have to deal with that issue again.

What I found, however, was that by repatterning that general category of *shame* (including all the permutations that have been laid out in this chapter), I then was able to see the next level of it, or some of the horizontal and vertical patterns that surrounded it. For example, I found that one of my beliefs was *that to be a woman meant to have shame*...and that *to be sexual meant to have shame* or to *feel shameful*.

When I began writing this book, I repatterned *not wanting to write, being afraid to write, not sitting down to write, etc.* Then I discovered the patterns of *resisting writing*...even *telling myself it would be wrong to write something so powerful.* Later I discovered patterns of *not being in the flow of the writing, not being in sync with it,* and *of resisting being in the flow and in sync with it.* Still later, I discovered patterns of *not wanting to complete the book*...of *dragging my heels*...of *wanting to drag it out.*

Again, whatever words I was using to describe how I was feeling, in the moment, was the next layer of pattern that was surfacing for me to remove.

Your Life as Your Workshop

As you already may have surmised, once you start working

with *Essence Repatterning*, you will find that your life becomes your workshop, your laboratory for discovering what specific limiting patterns stand between you and your next steps toward freedom, empowerment, happiness, effectiveness, competency, ease, fulfillment, prosperity...whatever the issue, it is right in front of you in that moment.

Again, I suggest that you be gentle—and patient—with yourself as you begin using this process. As discussed earlier, we have each been riding around in *our* particular horse-drawn carriage for more than a few years, and possibly decades.

You can trust that, *if* you are doing the process, you are being led to those patterns, experiences, and additional approaches that will help free you in the perfect timing...and at the perfect rate for you, wherever you are right now in your life.

Of course, if you are *not* being gentle, patient, and trusting of your process and timing, these are *simply* limiting patterns, ripe for reframing.

The next chapter will show you how to take this taste of *Essence Repatterning* and turn it into an easy, perhaps daily, feast for the true You, the part of you that has yearned to know how to take charge of your life, to effect change, and to have more of what you want—and deserve.

5

How to Begin
Essence Repatterning....

The focus of this chapter is twofold:
1) To help you begin working with Essence Repatterning—and your ego—in such a way that you can begin making some of the changes that, up until now, have been unattainable; and
2) To suggest a format that will enable you to make the most efficient use of Essence Repatterning in creating the major changes you desire and in repatterning the everyday annoyances and issues that may arise.

Part I. How Are You Feeling?

The shifts you have made thus far in reading this book undoubtedly have given you another perspective on this process called *Essence Repatterning*. Some of these new perspectives might be reflections of your ego, while others may be reflections of your true Self. How do you tell the difference?

One way is to notice any discomfort you might be feeling. If there is any sense, subtle or otherwise, of feeling or thinking that you are in danger... threatened....out of control...or in dangerous territory—that may be your ego. It, indeed, may be feeling *some* or *all* of those ways.

(If it isn't, that's fine too. At this point most people are excited at the prospect of applying this approach to their lives—

and it is possible to be feeling both the excitement and *also* the ego's fears. In fact, that is most common. Personally, every time I have gone to the next level of depth and truth within myself, I have found yet another layer of ego resistance to repattern.)

The way you can tell if you are experiencing your true Self is to notice the *rightness* of the feeling. Does it seem to be coming out of *truth*, or fear? Out of reaction, or *knowing*? If it seems to be coming out of truth or knowing, it is probably coming from your true Self. If it is coming out of fear or reaction, that is probably the ego.

The Ego Is Not the Enemy

It is important to remember that the ego is just trying to do its job—which it believes is to maintain the status quo and not rock the boat…even if the boat has some holes in it and you are, in fact, up to your ankles in water.

I say this so that you will remember that your ego is not your enemy. It is a part of you, an important part, that simply is working in accordance with some outdated programming—much of which was installed when you were very young. Each time you identify some of this old programming and reframe it, you are, in fact, giving your ego new, updated values and criteria for how it can best support you.

> Note: The terms, *reframe, repattern,* and *remove* patterns, will be used interchangeably throughout the rest of this book.

But perhaps you are not sure of the *rightness* of what you are feeling. That *uncertainty* can be addressed as a limiting pattern.

Let's begin listing some of the limiting patterns that have been mentioned so far. As we do this, notice that we are again beginning the *Essence Repatterning* process, in the moment, with where you are right now, and with what you are experiencing with this breath.

As I list these limiting patterns, I'm going to start from the beginning of this chapter and list the ones that have been mentioned. If you like, check me out and see if I have missed any, or if any others are triggered for you that you want to put on your list to repattern. (Again, use your words to describe what you see, feel, or hear as you read this.)

Pattern: Feeling discomfort
P: Thinking I'm in danger
P: Feeling threatened
P: Feeling out of control
P: Feeling I'm in dangerous territory
P: Experiencing ego resistance
P: Fear of the process
P: Fear of change
P: Being reactive to change
P: Not being sure of the rightness of what I'm feeling

Note: You can use *any* particular verb—*feeling, believing, thinking,* etc.—as you are listing your patterns. (It is not necessary to try and figure out: "Is it a belief or is it a feeling?" You are fully covered because, when you use the process on pages 46-47, you are including *all* of the other permutations for reframing.)

You will notice that I included *fear of the process* and *fear of change*. These seemed to be two obvious horizontal patterns related to the ones specifically articulated. (They are also generic limiting patterns that may come up any time you are learning something new—especially if it is something that is going to provoke significant change.)

Additional Mileage

What other patterns come to mind as you look at each of those listed? If you want to get additional mileage out of this chapter, you can take a few minutes now and add those to your list of patterns to reframe.

> ## RIPE FOR REFRAMING
>
> Again, *any* pattern that occurs to you is ripe for reframing. In fact, there are patterns you wouldn't think of now that, two months from now, you might see if you looked at this list again. The reason for this is that you will only think of, or notice, those patterns that are right and proper, *right now*, for you to identify and remove.
>
> As you work with this process, you are making yourself more and more available to the support, and useful information, that your unconscious has to offer. If you listen, it will tell you what would be useful to reframe, i.e., those patterns that are holding you back or making you feel stuck. The more you work with this, the more you will notice this happening. As people begin using *Essence Repatterning,* they typically report becoming more aware of their limiting patterns...and feeling more and more empowered as they reframe them and watch the changes unfold.

If you've written down all of the patterns you want to for the moment, notice if you are feeling ready to reframe them, or if you want to add more to the list before you do that. If you think you would be more comfortable *without* the patterns you've listed (and also the ones we've identified thus far in this chapter), take a few minutes now and repattern all of them using the process you learned in the last chapter—on pages 46-47.

"This Is Too Easy"

Perhaps one of the thoughts going through your mind now is: "This can't work; it's too easy." If so, you have just identified the next limiting patterns to address.

What are some other thoughts that come up?

Perhaps you believe that this won't work for you, or the classic: "Everyone else will get it but me."

What are some other ways that you might articulate limiting beliefs or feelings in these areas? The more patterns you can identify about not trusting yourself...the process...the unconscious...even God (believe it or not), the more freedom you will give yourself to fully explore the potential this process offers you for effecting significant change in your life.

If there's any belief that things *shouldn't* be this easy...or that certainly significant *change* shouldn't be this easy, you can add those beliefs to your list to be reframed. In fact, I suggest that you mine this territory as thoroughly as you can at this point. If you sincerely want to give yourself a clear shot at making this work for you, it will be helpful, and necessary, to defuse the ego of as many considerations, fears, and excuses as it may bring up for *not* doing the process and *not* moving forward.

"I'll Never *Get* It"

I know one Essence Repatterner, Brad, who, once he learned the process, spent the next couple of days working with patterns specifically and exclusively around these three basic issues:

P: *Believing it's too easy...*
P: *Believing it can't work...*
P: *Believing he would never "get" it...*

Brad knew that he had a pattern of *initially getting excited about something, but setting it up ultimately to feel disappointed and have his expectations dashed.* (Interestingly, he noticed that this was true not only with regard to opportunities for personal growth, but in relationships as well.)

After he reframed these patterns, he then saw that he had a pattern of *being attracted to approaches that didn't work*...or didn't work over the long haul...or perhaps it was that *he* didn't work them. Whatever the truth was for any particular situation, he knew that all of those patterns were being played out at one time or another.

As Brad reframed these and many other patterns, he found it easier to trust himself, the process, and also the decisions he was making in his personal life and on the job. Today, in addition to his work as an association director, Brad is also a trained *Essence Repatterning* practitioner who works with individuals to help them identify their limiting patterns.

If any of Brad's patterns have elicited an "aha" of recognition for you, you can put those patterns on-line by adding them to your to-be-reframed list. These patterns are golden. I have learned that any patterns you can reframe in the territories we've been discussing can be "money in the bank" for you, your emotional bank for sure and probably your financial, spiritual, and health accounts as well. As you reframe patterns in these areas, you will be giving yourself the freedom and support to use not only this process, but other effective processes as well, in ways that may bring you riches you have not yet imagined. There are people who are doing this. Why shouldn't you?

Fear of Being Too Powerful

That last question alone might bring up the next layer of limiting patterns. What does your ego think about you being that powerful? That successful? That fulfilled? If there are any limiting thoughts or beliefs that come up, I suggest you write them down. They, too, are money in the bank...because they are some of the patterns that keep you from having those specific results.

Let's explore some of the limiting patterns that might be in this territory:

>P: *Fear of being so powerful*
>P: *Fear of my own power*
>P: *Fear that if I am as powerful as I can be that I will be alone...isolated...separate...unloved... unliked*

> or disapproved of…disregarded…untouchable, etc.
> P: Belief that I shouldn't be more powerful than my mother/father were
> P: Belief that I should be small, unseen, unheard
> P: Belief that I should be helpless…that I am helpless
> P: Belief that I must stay a child…must not grow up
> P: Belief that I need someone else's authority to run my life

…And this is just the beginning! If you are serious about making significant shifts in your life, you probably will find more. But that may be enough for now in that territory. In fact, it may be time to reframe again. One way that I can tell that it is time for me to reframe is that things start feeling a little thick to me, as if the air has become heavier.

If you are feeling that it is time to dump this load of limiting patterns (everything that has been put on-line since the last time you reframed), simply turn to pages 46-47 and follow the process to remove these patterns.

Once you have done this, you may notice the next layer to be identified. Or you may find that it is time to put the book down and do something else for awhile. I urge you to honor your own timing and process. This work can feel intense at times. You are doing a lot as you identify limiting patterns and remove them. I suggest that you acknowledge that and be gentle with yourself.

What's Next?

In this process, when you are wondering "What's next?"…you only have to go as far as your ego's next negative, or doubt-provoking, or undermining thought. In this instance, perhaps it is telling you that *Essence Repatterning* is too good to be true….too weird…too hard to learn…that it's for *other* people….against natural laws….or anything else. Let's add those to the list:

> P: Believing/fearing that Essence Repatterning is too good to be true

P: Believing it's too weird
P: Believing/fearing that it's too hard to learn
P: Believing it's for other people, but not me
P: Believing/fearing that it's against natural laws

As you begin noticing what you are thinking or feeling right now, in the moment, you will uncover more and more self-talk, the chatter inside your head, much of which is negative. You can write down any of this negative self-talk as limiting patterns. Remember, a limiting pattern can be a belief, fear, assumption, thought, action, behavior, addiction, the way you're treated, the way you treat others, the way you feel about yourself, the things you tell yourself, and lots more.

In the next chapter, you will have an opportunity to deal in more depth with the general territory of *resistance to change.*

Part II. How to Make *Essence Repatterning* a Natural Part of Life

If you are sincere about change, it will be necessary to start by changing your priorities. Again, **if you always *do* what you've always done, you'll always *get* what you've always gotten.**

Whoever coined that phrase spoke the truth. One way to demonstrate to the ego that it's time for a change is by changing how we spend our time. For example, say you know someone who is unhappy with specific areas of her life, so unhappy, in fact, that she has decided to take the time she normally spends *complaining* about how his life is and how she is treated and use that time, instead, to *reframe* those patterns? That would mean that she has decided to invest some of her valuable time in herself, her empowerment, and in creating a better future for herself (and those she loves).

Do you think her ego might come up with reasons to sabotage that decision? Yes. But what if she used any pattern of *not* following these new priorities and *reframed* it, every time her ego came up with a new, more creative, rational, and convincing reason to do something else...anything else, but identify and remove limiting patterns.

Remember, every time she reframes even one pattern, and all the permutations listed on pages 46-47, she is automatically letting go of more of those old *rules for life* and giving herself permission to live according to values that are more current for her, values that go *beyond* survival toward thriving.

If this speaks to you, on the next two pages is a simple, daily routine you can adapt to your own needs. By following this, you will be automatically giving yourself a daily time for reflection—and connection with what you *want*, and with what's *not* working. Furthermore, you will begin routinely clearing out the debris of the past that no longer serves you and begin creating a new life that reflects more of what you truly deserve.

SETTING A TIME

If you decide to make using *Essence Repatterning* a priority, you may decide to do the process first thing in the morning as many people do (it can be a great way to start the day, fresh and clear); at night before you go to bed to clear out the day; even during a long bus or subway commute (and re-pattern your way to work each day).

If you don't have or know a convenient time to devote to re-patterning your life, you could address that *not knowing* as a limiting pattern and reframe it.

Daily Repatterning

1. Each day set aside a regular time to <u>write down</u> as limiting patterns:
   a. Any *general* qualities/experiences/aspects of your life that you don't like. For example:
      P: *Feeling unappreciated*
      P: *Feeling overwhelmed*
      P: *Feeling underpaid*

   Note: If the same thing seems to come up again later, it means there's another, similar pattern to reframe. To do this, simply find a new way of expressing it. In the examples above, it might be:
      P: *Feeling unsupported*
      P: *Feeling stressed out*
      P: *Feeling financial lack, or not having enough money*

   b. Any *specific* irritations or annoyances you have been experiencing, such as:
      P: *Feeling overlooked by my boss today*
      P: *Worrying about the funny sound my car is making*
      P: *Having a car that is not running well*
      P: *Feeling overwhelmed by everything I have to do*
      P: *Having children who are not keeping their agreements with me*

   c. Include as limiting patterns <u>not having</u> whatever it is that you desire. For example:
      P: **Not** *working at a job I like or love*
      P: **Not** *having a loving, fulfilling relationship*
      P: **Not** *having ample money to meet my wants and needs*
      P: **Not** *having a well-running car I am pleased with*

   d. Add to your list any <u>other patterns</u> you want to clear right now.

2. <u>Remove these limiting patterns</u> by following the process on pages 46-47.

3. <u>Use band-aid *Essence Repatterning*</u>, in the moment, when things are not going the way you want them to—*and* you don't have time to do the Basic *Essence Repatterning* process:
   a. Notice the limiting pattern, i.e., any negative circumstances. For example:
      P: *Being anxious in the middle of a meeting*
      P: *Being scared during a presentation, or as you are walking up to give one*
      P: *Feeling unconfident as you talk to a car salesman*
   b. Remove the pattern(s), *in the moment*, by making the reframing choice:
      "I choose to reframe these patterns and all allied limiting patterns now—and to know it."
   c. Since this quick approach will *not* remove any of the *other permutations* of these specific patterns (as listed on pages 46-47), you can clear these *all* out later by doing the whole Basic *Essence Repatterning* process on whatever limiting patterns you removed in the short term.
      <u>Note:</u> If you were to have such a challenging day that you found yourself using the band-aid process 20 or more times that day, what a powerful time that could be! It would mean that you were regularly redirecting your ego out of those old ways and patterns of being. In effect, you would be giving your ego a crash-course in how you want to be handling stress, what you deserve, and who's in charge.

4. <u>Claim your changes</u>...notice the changes, subtle, and otherwise, that begin occurring in your personal and work life.

The next chapter will discuss how limiting patterns may play out in specific areas of your life. It will offer some tips and directions to follow in identifying some of the obvious—and not so obvious—patterns that may prevent you from experiencing the next level of fulfillment, ease, and success for which you are ready.

6

Specific Applications

This chapter explores:
1) Three fundamental areas of limiting patterns that affect one's success in all other areas;
2) Five Standard Limiting Patterns that can be found in any situation; and
3) Suggestions regarding how to apply Essence Repatterning principles to four basic areas of life.

The more *Essence Repatterning* that you do, the more you will be freeing yourself from the limiting patterns that have been keeping you stuck or holding you back. Fortunately, you don't have to take anyone else's word for this. You can demonstrate it for yourself.

As each of us identifies our limiting patterns, layer by layer, and removes them, we are dissolving the false beliefs, *shoulds*, and self-sabotaging behaviors that have inhibited us from expressing our true strengths, wisdom, and clarity.

In this chapter we are going to examine some useful approaches to dealing with limiting patterns in several specific, everyday areas of life. To begin, however, I'm going to focus on three fundamental areas that often have a major impact on all of the others. By addressing some of the limiting patterns in these areas first, you will be giving yourself an advantage in working with others later in this chapter.

These three fundamental areas are:
- Resistance to change
- Claiming your power
- Self-Esteem issues

As you begin reframing limiting patterns around these topics, you will be laying the groundwork, and making it easier, to deal later in the chapter with patterns that relate to finances, relationships, career, and health.

For example, if you are resisting change...or resisting claiming your power...or have low self-esteem...then it will be very difficult to deal effectively with the outer manifestations of those limiting patterns, which are what our finances, relationships, career, and health often reflect. By removing the first layer of limitation in these areas, you will be making it easier to move forward—and also learning about some key areas to address as you are doing *Essence Repatterning* on your own.

Resistance to Change

We began working with the issue of *resistance to change* in the last chapter, specifically as it related to learning *Essence Repatterning*. Now let's take a deeper look at it within a broader context.

Every ego resists change. As we've discussed, change is perceived as a threat by the ego because it is attached, even addicted, to maintaining the status quo. It believes that its life depends on it.

Personally, I used to believe that I loved change. The truth is that I was titillated by the prospect of change. By focusing on the future and possible changes that *might* occur, I kept myself out of the present, out of being more fully available to possible enjoyment in the *here and now*, and—especially—I kept myself out of my power. For if I wasn't fully present, it was difficult to be grounded and experiencing my innate power. And experiencing my power was definitely a no-no while I was growing up. But, of course, all of these limiting patterns supported my ego's belief in *the natural order of things*, and the *rules for life*, that I learned as a child.

After all, as children, how many times did we receive consistent, reinforcing support for us expressing our power? Right or wrong, the focus usually was on urging us to "be good," "make mommy happy," or to "not make daddy mad."

So, if you are hearing a little voice inside say, "But I love change," or "I love being powerful," consider the source. Listen for the truth. If you have any doubt whatsoever regarding whether or not these basic limiting patterns apply to you, I encourage you to err on the side of assuming that they might be yours, even if it's just a little. In that way, you will remove whatever remnant, or layer, of the pattern that may apply to you now.

By the way, when I use the word *power*, what *I* mean by that and how my *ego* may hold that are often two different things. When I refer to claiming *your power*, or your *innate* power, I am referring to the power of your true Self, the power that comes out of an alignment with the highest within us. This is usually different than being *in control* or being *in charge*, which is the kind of power to which the ego can relate.

What are some of the horizontal/vertical patterns that might surround the pattern of *being resistant to change*? As you read the following list, I encourage you to be open to seeing, or hearing, or feeling out, some additional patterns that speak to you, patterns that are ripe for reframing and which will free you to move forward more easily.

- P: *Being resistant to change*
- P: *Being afraid, scared, terrified of change*
- P: *Believing that change is bad, dangerous, painful and awful*
- P: *Being afraid to rock the boat...believing that if I do, I will be hurt*
- P: *Being afraid to do anything "mommy/daddy" wouldn't approve of* (**Note:** *Whether or not it is true that they would* not *approve does not seem to matter.*

The subconscious has been shown to retain these early beliefs even if they are no longer relevant...or accurate.)

P: *Believing that if I change, it will be for the worse*
P: *Believing that no one will love me if I change*
P: *Believing that I have to keep myself stuck to be loved*
P: *Believing that if I am not "broken", I will be different, and that if I am different, I won't fit in, or be loved*
P: *Believing that God doesn't want me to change*
P: *Believing that whatever circumstances I had as a child is what God wants me to have now*
P: *Believing that I don't deserve 'good' change, only 'bad' change*

If you sense that more limiting patterns are there for you, continue writing them down. You can always resume reading when you are done.

Take Care of Yourself

Also, remember to take care of yourself. If it is time to reframe the patterns that you've written down, or those that you've been reading in this or other chapters, do that now. Turn to pages 46-47, and follow the reframing process there. Then come back to this chapter when you are ready to continue.

There is no hurry. The next area for exploration will still be there whenever you return after reframing these patterns and taking the time—anywhere from a few minutes to even a few days—to integrate the changes you have been putting into motion.

However, if you find yourself valuing what you are learning about *Essence Repatterning,* and *not* using it, or not continuing to read and learn about the process, then you may have a limiting pattern of *not doing what it takes to move forward...*or *sabo-*

taging yourself. (In fact, you also could reframe: *not reading the book*...and *not using the process.*)

These are common limiting patterns. If you find them playing out in this instance, they undoubtedly play out in others. In any event, if you suspect that they, or any others like them, are in there, you can add them to your list to reframe.

We have identified a few of the patterns that relate to *resistance to change.* If you sit quietly, with pen and paper in hand, and ask what others you are ready to identify, you undoubtedly will hear what some of those are. (If you don't hear what some of them are the first time you ask, try again later. You may have to build some credibility with yourself if you are not accustomed to sitting quietly and asking for inner guidance. However, that guidance *is* there and you *will* open to it. Of course, if you are *not* opening to it, that's just a limiting pattern too...and you can reframe: *not being open to my inner guidance...inner wisdom...and inner support.*

Claiming Your Power

Now that you've begun identifying some limiting patterns in the area of bei*ng resistant to change,* let's start identifying some of the ways people commonly *resist claiming their power.*

If you had a dominating parent or guardian, it can be easy to see the ways you may have learned *not* to claim your power. However, sometimes the domination is more subtle. If a child is constantly criticized, made fun of, or reminded that he or she is not measuring up to some standard, that child very often will grow up believing he/she does not have what it takes and is, in fact, a loser.

These negative, stultifying influences are not limited to the home, however. They are prevalent in our schools and in our culture in general.

Being Undervalued

One example of this is Bill, a very intelligent, clever man of 6'5" who is now in his late 50s. When he was a teenager, he vividly remembers being noticed or valued in school only when the nuns needed furniture moved. Looking back now, he realizes that he apparently bought into an assumption *that anyone that big could not be intelligent.*

Although today he *intellectually* knows better, if you look at his life as a whole, it is clear that that limiting belief has been a *rule for life* that has inhibited him from fully claiming and expressing his power. Although he was always a quick study and his parents had the money to put him through college, he dropped out of college after one year. In later years he often talked in wistful terms about the marketing strategies he learned there, as if he really would have liked to pursue a career in that field.

Because of the diminished expectations that were communicated to him—and which he internalized, he put himself into jobs that never really challenged him, settling for a modicum of success, but never really giving his all in a way that would reflect his brilliance. It is as if he felt *no permission* to claim and express who he really is.

In Bill's case, he actually was handicapped by being tall...or, more accurately, by his teachers' perceptions of what that implied about him and his capabilities. In the case of Edwin, another highly intelligent man who is in his 40s, his *perceived handicap* has been being black, being an African-American.

Because of the limiting messages he internalized as a child from his personal family culture, and from the all-encompassing general culture, regarding *what is possible* for a young black boy, Edwin has kept his sphere of influence very small. By internalizing his *father's* low self-esteem and his father's belief that he, himself, didn't have what it takes, Edwin also told himself that *he* didn't have what it takes—even though he does.

Of course, Edwin's father probably was only believing what *his* father may have believed and taught him, all of which was highly influenced by cultural messages about *how life is* and by their real experience of those messages.

Now, however, using *Essence Repatterning*, Edwin is seeing that he does not have to accept the prevailing negative cultural messages about blacks, and especially black men, being disempowered.

Although he and his wife, Terry, have created a good life for themselves and their family, they have done it in a way that has been harder than it had to be and in ways that resulted in them always *feeling under-the-gun financially*. When I met them in an *Essence Repatterning* seminar, Edwin was working as a courier, and she worked at a bank. Together they cleaned office buildings during the weekend as part of the janitorial business they started to earn extra money.

In Edwin's first individual *Essence Repatterning* session, we discovered stored in his subconscious many limiting patterns around *being and feeling* (and this is how it was specifically worded)...*controlled and victimized by racism, unfair standards and rules,* and *"whitey"*. In that session, he also discovered that he had learned specific *rules for life* that *required him to lose, to sabotage himself, to hold himself back* and *to stifle his true genius and brilliance.*

Today, Edwin is beginning to turn his life around. While he knows that societal prejudice and racism are still realities of life, he is no longer holding some of these issues as *rules for life,* as *the way life has to be.* As he continues to reframe subsequent layers of these patterns, he is finding additional, often more subtle, ones in this general territory.

Edwin and Terry both feel as if they have a new lease on life. It is not that everything is wonderful for them, but that, when it is not, they now have specific tools they can use to actively address the problems that arise.

> One sign of Edwin's progress is that presently he is dealing with financial obligations that had been hanging over his head, and holding him back, for a long time. Another indication of progress for both Edwin and Terry is that they are planning to give up their janitorial business and start something that is more in alignment with their new sense of expanded confidence and potential.

Inherent in both of these examples are some implicit limiting patterns we *all* share of *living in a society in which people are undervalued...in which people are judged, not for who they are but based upon such issues as race, sex, religious preference, sexual preference, ethnic origin, and physical appearance*, to name a few. (If you like, you can add such limiting patterns to your list to reframe, as well as any other societal patterns you notice for yourself.)

By the way, one way to use the above examples, no matter how tall you are or what color your skin, is to substitute for those so-called handicaps the words or adjectives that you have allowed—or used—to deny your power and keep yourself feeling helpless or out of control. When we are feeling out of control, that is a sign that we have given our power to forces outside of ourselves, or that we believe that forces outside of ourselves are more powerful than we are. Either way, these patterns are reflections of ways in which we are not claiming our innate power and actively directing our own lives.

Now some readers might feel that I just questioned a *sacred cow* when I implied that it is a limiting pattern to *believe that forces outside of us are more powerful than we are.* If this belief is one of your hard-and-fast *rules for life*, it may be one of the key ways, perhaps even a *meta-pattern* (a limiting pattern that pervades your whole life and colors every aspect of it), that your ego uses to keep you feeling disempowered.

Since this is a very common limiting pattern, I am going to begin with it as we start listing some of the specific patterns connected with *not claiming our power.* (Again I encourage you to add to your personal reframing list any additional patterns that these provoke for you. Also, I remind you to do the repatterning process on pages 46-47 when you feel that you are ready.)

> P: *Belief that forces outside of me are more powerful than I am*
> P: *Belief/feeling that I am a leaf in the wind*
> P: *Belief that I have to be weak...that is how my father/mother was, and that is what I must be*
> P: *Belief that I won't be liked or loved if I am strong and/or powerful*
> P: *Belief that power is bad...corrupt*
> P: *Belief that I will be bad/corrupt if I am powerful*
> P: *Belief that power is evil and that only evil people are powerful*
> P: *Belief that I must stuff my power...deny it...pretend it isn't there*
> P: *Belief that my mother/father will abandon me if I am powerful...or if I am as powerful as them, or more powerful than them*
> P: *Belief that I will be killed if I'm too powerful*
> P: *Belief that I will be imprisoned...jailed, if I express my power*
> P: *Belief that my life depends upon pretending to be weak, helpless and powerless*
> P: *Feeling scared of my own power*
> P: *Feeling scared of others' power*
> P: *Believing others have power over me*
> P: *Believing that I must sabotage my power...and keep myself small*

When you have identified as many limiting patterns as you can for now around the issue of power...*not claiming your power...or stuffing it,* take a few minutes and reframe all of these patterns and any others you've identified by following the process on pages 46-47.

Self-Esteem

Of all the areas we have discussed, the one that probably has the greatest influence, across the board, on the quality of our lives, is that of self-esteem—the degree to which we value ourselves. The extent to which we *truly* value ourselves is reflected in the quality of life we are presently experiencing. Of course, this does not mean that someone with a million-dollar home necessarily has high self-esteem...or that someone living in more humble circumstances has low self-esteem.

The quality of life I am referring to is that of our inner life, the place where we meet *ourselves*, the place where we truly live. I imagine that each person reading this book knows of someone, or has heard or read of someone, who lives very humbly, and who also demonstrates a sense of deep inner peace and oneness with himself or herself. To me, this is true self-esteem. It is something to which many of us aspire.

What I have found is that, when we access the truth of what *runs* us, what motivates us, the same kinds of limiting patterns are often at play—for those who *have* material wealth...and for those who *do not have* material wealth. Admittedly, it looks different on the surface and, in fact, some of the upper layers of limiting patterns may be substantially different, but underneath all that, the core self-esteem issues are often the same.

For example, someone who has substantial wealth may believe that she has to prove herself—actually try and prove her value, by having a big house or a flashy car. Interestingly enough, another individual who is living a middle-class lifestyle may be living according to the same *rules for life*, but on a different scale. Perhaps he did not grow up in a middle-class family, but in a blue-collar family. In this case, being middle-class is one way he may try to prove himself.

In these examples, the focus is not on how these patterns play out, but on the patterns themselves. From my perspective, it is one thing for someone to work hard and earn enough to pay for the finer things in life because she *likes the work* she is doing—

and because she simply likes living the good life. That is coming out of free choice.

It is another thing to work hard and buy those things because she believes she *has to*...in this example, because she believes she *has to prove that she is o.k.*, or *worthwhile*.

To me, anytime we work hard just to *disprove* a limiting belief, we are working hard for the *wrong* reason. Instead, why not just start repatterning limiting beliefs in these areas and see what happens?

So far, we have been exploring how this might play out for those who *have* abundance; let's look now at how it may play out for those who *don't* have abundance.

Just as those who *have* abundance often are motivated by a belief that they are *not o.k.*, or *not enough* just as they are, those who do *not have* as much of the good life as they desire usually are demonstrating, and living, those same beliefs. In the example of Edwin (cited earlier in this chapter), he grew up believing that he was not enough, that *who* he was and *how* he was, was unacceptable. In his case, the way his *rules* were written required him to demonstrate this by *not* living too well...and not being too successful. Consequently, he has been expending a considerable amount of energy inhibiting, and undercutting, his natural abilities and ambition to excel.

It has been my experience that the particular way in which this pattern had been playing out with Edwin is common for people who have been living *beneath their potential*. Furthermore, I have found that it is often tied in with a pattern of having a mother/father who also lived *beneath his or her potential*.

For me, personally, it was an eye-opener to discover that I had a pattern of believing that I *should be a ne'er-do-well*. In other words, I had a pattern of believing that I *should never really amount to much*. Sure, I could get close, but not too close, to real success. If I did, there was always a seemingly rational reason to change direction or sabotage myself in some way.

As I explored the beliefs stored in my subconscious, I found that this pattern was an outgrowth of the way my father was portrayed to me as I was growing up. Since my parents divorced when I was about three, my father was not around much (until I went to live with him as a teenager). However, whenever he was mentioned, as is the case with many divorced partners, it usually was with some disparagement.

Unbeknownst to me, I internalized this *way of being*, my father's way of being (or how he was perceived to be), as one of my *rules for life*. While I didn't know him well at that point, he was, after all, my father, the man from whom I came. Perhaps out of a need to belong and feel connected to him, I somehow chose to identify with him in the only way I could at that point, which was in how he was portrayed to me.

As I grew older, I learned that there were other aspects I received from my father as well. In my '30s, I began to appreciate his deeply spiritual nature and also the degree to which that is an important part of my heritage.

(However, that had its downside, too. I now realize that the deep-seated patterns I have uncovered in myself of believing that *you cannot have too much money and still be spiritual...or be a good person...*reflect the messages my father gave me when I was living with him as a teenager.)

Sound Familiar?

If any of this rings true for you, in terms of taking on limiting characteristics (true or otherwise) from one or both of your parents, you can add these patterns to your list to reframe. All you need to do is substitute *your* descriptive words for my old *ne'er-do-well* pattern...and also the patterns of *needing to feel disparaged...*or *criticized*.

The self-esteem issues we've been discussing are a natural part of the territory in which people work when they do *Essence Repatterning*. Whatever one's bank balance is, as he removes the patterns that limit his self-esteem, layer by layer, he automatically is setting a new inner direction toward values that are more in alignment with his essence. (Incidentally, this usually results in more financial ease as well.)

It doesn't matter if it is someone who has been a) working hard to prove himself by being a successful financial planner, or b) working hard, just to make ends meet, within a very constricted set of rules that prohibit him from easily being successful. As he reframes, the new *inner* direction he is setting is consistently toward what he truly wants to be doing. This is evident in the new values he starts expressing and in the new work he begins moving toward and embracing.

We've probably all read and heard about people who have chucked it all—walked away from what they thought they *should* be doing—and begun doing what they really *wanted* to do. I've heard story after story about how, as people do this, the money just naturally comes. There's even a book called, *Do What You Love, The Money Will Follow,* by Marsha Sinetar.

With *Essence Repatterning,* you can remove the patterns of *doing what you* ***don't*** *love,* ***not*** *doing what you do love,* and also any beliefs *that you can't make money doing what you really love.* (Later in this chapter I will talk more about how to apply *Essence Repatterning* to career issues.)

Just now, let's begin listing some of the limiting patterns that have come up in the area of self-esteem and see what additional ones emerge.

    P: *Believing I have to prove myself*
    P: *Believing/feeling that I'm not enough*
    P: *Believing/feeling that I'm not o.k....that there is something wrong with me*
    P: *Believing/feeling that I'm bad*
    P: *Believing/feeling that I'm worthless*

Remember, if these patterns are in your subconscious even the least bit, they can hold you back. Furthermore, I have not worked with anyone who did not demonstrate, through muscle-testing, both the presence of these limiting patterns at one stage or another—and the body/spirit's desire to remove them.

If there is any resistance to including these patterns in your own reframing, guess who that might be coming from? The ego obviously may not relish giving up these familiar limiting patterns.

What are some of the other patterns that can diminish self-esteem and hold us back?

> P: Believing/feeling that I am broken...that I need to be fixed
> P: Believing/feeling that I am no good...perhaps deeply stained
> P: Believing/feeling that I am a good-for-nothing
> P: Believing/feeling that I am _____
> *(fill in the blank with whatever negative names or words that you have been called, that you call yourself, that you call others, or that you simply think of or hear in your head as you read this.)*

At this point, you might feel a little heavy. Whether you realize it or not, you have put a lot of limiting patterns on-line. I suggest that you take a few minutes now and reframe all of the patterns that have come up since your last reframing. (Follow the Basic *Essence Repatterning* process on pages 46-47.)

By the way, the words you hear to fill in the blank above may surprise you. Write them down anyway. These words represent the limiting beliefs that your unconscious is saying you are ready to remove. Each time you reread this particular section of the chapter, you probably will hear different words to fill in. Again, it is a layer-by-layer process.

It is interesting to note that whatever names we use to put down others are actually the names *we* have been called or that we call ourselves in our self-talk. These represent some of our limiting beliefs about ourselves. (**Hint:** Notice the adjectives you hurl at other drivers on the road if you are cut off or treated rudely. They come from this subconscious reservoir as well and can be reframed.)

As each of these limiting beliefs and feelings is identified and removed, you will find it easier to be more of who you truly are and to feel deserving of what you truly want.

Quick Results

As you begin, or proceed on your own with *Essence Repatterning*, one way to see results quickly is to regularly sit down, pen and paper at hand, and ask yourself:

What's the next layer of limiting pattern to remove in the areas of:

    1) Resistance to change
    2) Not claiming my power
    3) Self-esteem...or not feeling good about myself.

As you do this, along with identifying other patterns in your day-to-day activities, you will be taking charge of your life in ways that now you might not imagine are possible. You will see changes not only in yourself, but in those around you. You will find yourself treating others differently, and you will find others treating *you* differently—even people you don't know!

But I Don't *Know* What I Want

As we begin looking at some angles on how to identify limiting patterns in such areas as money, career, and relationships, you might realize that, in some areas, you just *don't know* what you want. You may know what you *don't* want, but perhaps you don't have a clue as to what you *do* want. No problem. If this is true for you (and it is for everyone at one time or another), you have just identified another limiting pattern.

    P: Not knowing what I want in the area
       of: _____

Then there probably are the related patterns of:

    P: Not wanting to know what I want
    P: Being afraid to know what I want

P: Believing/feeling that I shouldn't have what I want
P: Believing/feeling that, if I have what I want, I'll be punished
P: Believing/feeling that what I want isn't important
P: Believing/feeling that it would be dangerous to have what I want
P: Believing/feeling that my wants must come second (or last)
P: Believing/feeling that it is wrong to want
P: Believing/feeling that if I want something, I'll just be disappointed, so that it is better not to want and not to even know what I want
P: Believing that if I knew what I wanted, I might have it...and therefore that it is safer not to know what I want
P: Believing God doesn't want me to have what I want
P: Believing I'm not allowed to even have wants
P: Believing I don't deserve to have my needs met
P: Believing/feeling that I don't deserve to have needs...or wants

Before you proceed, please stop now and reframe these patterns, and any others you've identified since the last time you reframed. (See format on pages 46-47.)

Again, I urge you to do this at your own pace. If you wonder if you are doing too little at a time, or too much, you can work with that as a limiting pattern, too. Anything we don't know and want to know is a limiting pattern of:

P: Not knowing _____
P: Not wanting to know...
P: Being unwilling to know...
P: Having to doubt myself...and obscure my truth
P: Being afraid to know
P: Using 'not knowing' as a way to sabotage myself or hold myself back

As you reframe *not knowing* the proper pace for you, you will either a) relax into a pace you trust and *know* that you are doing fine, or b) see the next layer of pattern to reframe with regard to *not knowing*.

You may have wondered about the pattern of *not wanting* to know what is the appropriate pace for you, or the earlier suggested pattern of *not wanting* to know what you want. These patterns are included because, based upon my findings, whatever we have (or don't have) is exactly what our subconscious has concluded that we want—based upon the many limiting beliefs and patterns stored there. In other words, what we have (or don't have) is *what we believe we deserve.*

Five Standard Limiting Patterns

So if there is something that you want (and don't have), there are five standard limiting patterns with which you can begin to identify the blocks that keep you from having that result. These generic limiting patterns are:

- P: **Not having** the result you want
- P: **Not wanting** to have that result
- P: **Feeling unworthy** of having that result
- P: **Not doing what it takes** to have that result
- P: **Telling yourself that undesirable or awful things would happen** if you **did** have that result (*then identify what those things are and reframe believing these fears*)

The last pattern may be a surprise to you at first, but as you remove it, you probably will discover several things that you tell yourself that serve to keep you from having your stated result.

For example, say that you want a good (or great) relationship with a man/woman. If you don't now have that result you might discover that there is a limiting pattern of telling yourself that, if you did have a good relationship...*he/she would only leave you*...or that *it would never last*...or that *you'd have to spend a lot of money on them, and you can't afford it,* etc. Any of these beliefs or patterns could prevent you from having a good primary relationship.

Relationship Issues

What are some of the other limiting patterns that may be blocking someone from having a good relationship, or even a wonderful relationship, whatever that means?

First, I would begin by applying the Five Standard Limiting Patterns, just discussed, to the issue. Then you may find patterns of:

P: *Believing/feeling no one would have me*

P: *Believing/feeling I don't have what it takes to be in a good relationship*

P: *Believing/feeling that I am unattractive...too fat...too thin...too poor...too ugly...too (fill in the blank) _____*

P: *Believing/feeling that I'll never have someone I love*

P: *Believing/feeling that I am unlovable*

P: *Believing/feeling that how my mother/father treated me is how I'm supposed to be treated in an intimate relationship—**and** how I'm supposed to treat others in an intimate relationship*

P: *Believing/feeling that I am a loser*

P: *Believing/feeling that I am or have to be unsuccessful in relationships*

P: *Believing/feeling that my mother/father has to be my model for relationships*

P: *Believing/feeling that I can't have a better relationship than, or a different relationship than, my parents had*

Although some of these patterns may seem the same, they are not. The wording is different. Remember that the subconscious is *very literal* and that it is important to include *as many variations of wording as you can* in order to clear out as much of these limiting tendencies as possible.

Before you proceed, you may want to reframe the patterns you have put on-line since the last reframing.(Turn to pages 46-47.)

Once you have removed these patterns, and any others you can think of right now, you undoubtedly will notice the next layer of patterns to be addressed.

> ## Identifying the Next Pattern
>
> Remember, the way to identify the next pattern to be removed is to notice *what you are complaining about...*or *what you tell yourself, or others,* about a given situation. Use the exact wording of your complaint or description as the pattern to be reframed.
>
> Once you have reframed *that* description of the situation, you probably will describe it in different terms. That is the *next* pattern to remove.
>
> *Then* notice how you describe the problem. The terms you use then will be the *next* layer of pattern to remove.
>
> For example, if you are *not* in what you would term a good (or great) primary relationship and have removed the above patterns, notice the way you would describe the situation now—and reframe those patterns.

Perhaps you feel hopeless about ever having someone really love you. Perhaps, even, you are thinking that your mother was right when she said, "You're impossible to live with. You are selfish and only think of yourself." (Of course, you can include any words that you remember your mother/father/grandmother/teachers saying to you in a disparaging way.)

If there is anything like this that has come up, you can add that to your list of patterns to reframe:

> *P: Believing/feeling hopeless regarding ever having someone really love you*

> P: *Thinking my mother was right: I am impossible to live with...selfish...and only think of myself*

Once you've reframed those, you might notice patterns of *not liking yourself...feeling unliked by others...* and *feeling unlikeable* in general. Perhaps you also *feel unloved...undeserving of love...* and suspect, or realize, that you *don't truly love yourself.*

If we are not loving ourselves, how can we expect others to like, love, or accept us? As a diligent repatterner begins to remove these patterns, layer by layer, she will begin treating herself differently and also begin to notice a change in how others perceive and treat her as well.

Let's add these last patterns to the list:

> P: *Not liking myself*
> P: *Feeling unliked by others*
> P: *Believing/feeling that I am unlikeable*
> P: *Feeling unloved*
> P: *Feeling undeserving of love*
> P: *Not loving myself*
> P: *Not accepting myself...and/or rejecting myself*

Again, remember you can apply the Five Standard Limiting Patterns discussed earlier to any specific patterns you want to address more thoroughly.

Now notice if it is time for you to reframe. If it is, do so by following the format on pages 46-47.

Once you have removed these patterns, you might hear the word *undesirable* pop up. If so, there probably is a pattern of *feeling undesirable.* You can add that to your next list of patterns to be reframed.

Patterns That Involve Others

In the last chapter, one example I used dealt with *having children who are not keeping their agreements with you.* Notice that I phrased that situation very specifically in terms of *your* pattern. I could as easily have used examples of *having a mate who ignores you*, or *having a mother who treats you like a child*. The pattern is always *ours*, not theirs. Let's talk briefly about how to work with patterns that involve specific others.

The first thing to remember is that *the only patterns you can remove are your own*. However, as you correctly identify—and remove—your own limiting patterns that involve others, you will see changes in your interactions and experiences with them.

For example, if you have a pattern of *being mistreated by your boss* (or spouse), it is *your* pattern. This is not to say that it is a one-way street. Of course, if you are being mistreated, then it is obvious that someone is doing the mistreating. However, the most effective way for you to address the issue is to work with the patterns within *you*, the patterns that *require* that you be mistreated. As discussed in chapters 3 and 4, if someone is being mistreated, there is a pattern of believing that this is what he or she deserves.

To understand this more clearly, think of a way that you have felt mistreated as an adult. Then, think back to your childhood and remember times when you were mistreated and begin identifying some of those *rules for life*. As you identify and remove these *rules for life*, these limiting patterns (along with the horizontal/vertical variations discussed in Chapter 4), you will be removing the *pathways for being mistreated*. Then, if you are working with someone who has a pattern of mistreating others, it will not matter—for you will no longer have a pathway to attract, or allow, being mistreated. In fact, even as you start exploring the most obvious variations on this issue, and removing those patterns, you probably will see at least subtle shifts in your interactions with the individual involved. *You* will have created these shifts. When these shifts occur, it is because you have changed your patterns, and they are responding to your changes.

One example of this is Jim, a systems analyst at the Pentagon who, when we first worked together, was *feeling mistreated on the job*. After addressing this issue specifically, along with others involving low self-esteem, he reported significant positive changes within a few days of that session. These initial shifts helped him see other patterns he wanted to remove, and today he is experiencing a vastly improved work environment.

Money Issues

Although we began this part of the discussion with the topic of relationships—because it is key for so many people, we could as easily have begun with the topic of money. It's amazing how many people have money issues...regardless of their income, bank account, or financial standing. In fact, let's list that as our first limiting money pattern:

>P: Having money issues, money worries and anxieties.

Of course, any issues related to the three fundamental areas discussed at the beginning of the chapter (resistance to change...claiming our power...and self-esteem) have a direct impact on our money picture, as well.

As you begin considering limiting patterns in this area, I encourage you also to include the Five Standard Limiting Patterns. For example, say you have a pattern of *being in debt*...or *not having a good-paying job/business you really love*...or *not having the quality of life you desire.* (Of course, you can substitute any patterns in place of these three examples.)

In applying the Five Standard Limiting Patterns to the first of these specific money patterns, it would look like:

>P: **Being** in debt
>P: **Wanting** to be in debt
>P: **Feeling unworthy** of not being in debt
>P: **Not doing what it takes** to be out of debt
>P: **Telling myself that undesirable or awful things would happen** if I weren't in debt (*then identify what those things are and reframe believing these fears*)

Once you have applied these standard limiting patterns to the issue of *being in debt,* notice what other limiting patterns may be related to this. Perhaps:

    P: *Believing that being in debt is a way of life*
    P: *Believing that I must be in debt*
    P: *Believing that I must feel one-down, under the gun, less than everyone else*
    P: *Believing that being in debt is a badge of honor...that it makes me belong and be like other people*
    P: *Believing that God wants me to be in debt (after all, my parents were)*
    P: *Believing that there is not enough to go around*
    P: *Believing that I am a product of lack and, therefore, must live in lack (to one degree or another)*
    P: *Believing that if I had too much money, I would be ostracized or abandoned by those who love me*

Is it time to reframe the patterns you have put on-line? If so, do so now before continuing. (See pages 46-47 for the reframing process.)

Once you have dumped that load of limiting patterns, you obviously will see others, either now or later. When you do, simply add them to your list of patterns to reframe.

In working with the example of the second money issue cited above, that of *not having a good-paying job/business you really love...*again, begin with the Five Standard Limiting Patterns of:

    P: **Not having** a good-paying job/business you really love
    P: **Not wanting** to have a good-paying job/business you really love
    P: **Feeling unworthy** of having a good-paying job/business, etc.
    P: **Not doing what it takes** to have a good-paying job/business, etc.

P: **Telling myself that undesirable or awful things would happen** if I **did** have a good-paying job/business, etc.(*Then identify what those things are and reframe believing these fears.*)

Now that you have applied the Five Standard Limiting Patterns to this issue, it's time to think, feel out, or listen to hear what additional limiting patterns there are to include. Here are some examples:

P: *Telling myself that I can't have a better job...or financial picture...or job fulfillment than my mother/father did*

P: *Believing that I have to stay constricted and impeded and that if I were enjoying my job, or my life, it would be against the rules*

P: *Believing that life has to be hard...it is not to be enjoyed*

P: *Believing that work has to be drudgery*

P: *Believing that if I am enjoying myself too much I will be punished*

P: *Believing that it would be embarrassing to be so different from everyone I know...if I enjoyed my work*

P: *Believing that my survival depends on being like everyone else...even if it means sabotaging myself in order to not stand out*

Obviously, there are more patterns that will emerge once you have reframed this batch. If it is time to reframe, turn to pages 46-47.

Let's apply this same process to the third money example cited above. Starting with the Five Standard Limiting Patterns, we have:

P: **Not having** the quality of life I desire
P: **Not wanting** to have the quality of life I desire
P: **Feeling unworthy** of having the quality of life I desire

> P: **Not doing what it takes** to have the quality of life I desire
> P: **Telling myself that undesirable or awful things would happen** if I **did** have the quality of life I desire *(Then identify what those things are and reframe believing these fears.)*

Again, what are the additional limiting patterns that come up to add to your list in this particular territory? Some of them might include:

> P: *Telling myself that if I did have the quality of life I desire I would be greedy, egotistical, unbearable, and alone*
> P: *Believing that it is wrong to have more than other people*
> P: *Believing that if I have abundance, it means someone else has less*
> P: *Believing that there's not enough to go around*
> P: *Believing that I can't have mine until everyone else has theirs*
> P: *Believing I can't be spiritual* **and** *successful, or financially abundant*
> P: *Believing that it is wrong to be abundant...bad... immoral...and that I would be punished if I were*
> P: *Believing that money is dirty...and being rich is despicable*
> P: *Believing that wealthy people are evil and money-grubbing*

As you are noticing any other patterns to add to this list, you might add any old adages or popular myths about money that come to mind. I have found that those myths are, more times than not, imbedded in the subconscious as *rules for life*.

Some examples you might consider are the idea of being *filthy rich*, or believing that *money is the root of all evil*. Although the Bible often has been cited as the source of negative concepts about money, many people, including many members of the clergy, have concluded that these quotations have been misinterpreted.

Personally, I grew up in a consciousness of lack (there's a good pattern to reframe) and, as I have developed more inner fullness through the years, it has become clear to me that it is o.k. with God if I am happy...comfortable... live well, and enjoy the richness of being alive on this physical level. Note that I am *not* talking about doing any of this in an imbalanced, greedy, or grabby way. I *am* talking about *living* life fully, learning all there is here to learn, and getting the most out of this life opportunity—in ways that produce a *win-win-win* for all.

This is different from the *I win-you lose* approach and even goes beyond the *win-win* approach, in which we *both* win. I first learned of this concept a few years ago when I heard an environmentalist discuss the idea of *win-win-win*—where *you* win, *I* win, and that we do that in such a way that it is a win for *society* as well...so that an integral part of *our* win reflects a win for *all*, including the environment and our culture in general.

As I have realized that it is o.k. *not* to live out of lack, on any level, I have also concluded that perhaps the whole point of this life opportunity is to make the most of it...to give it our best shot...to do those things that bring us fulfillment in win-win-win ways...and to actually *thrive* in the process. Again, implicit in all of this is that it is not done in a way that *takes* from anyone else, but in ways that actually *add* to others— in other words, in ways that *support* our society and one another.

Career Issues

Let's move on to the area of career. We began addressing this in the last chapter and also in the discussion on money. This will deepen the process.

If you are in a job or career that feels as if it is a deadend...or boring...or doesn't stimulate or fulfill you...you are not alone. While that awareness may not comfort you, it *may* help you to know that most of the people who feel that way undoubtedly believe that *that is how life is*, i.e., you work in a deadend job...or a boring one...or one that doesn't fulfill you. *That's life*. (In other words, those are the *rules*.)

The good news for you is that, with *Essence Repatterning*, you now have a specific approach you can use to change these beliefs and limiting patterns. In that respect, you are uniquely different from most other people. If you apply *Essence Repatterning* to your job and career issues, most likely you will, as so many others have, begin to open to unexpected opportunities and to feel inspired and empowered by the changes you are creating in your life.

To begin, I'm going to use the limiting pattern just stated, that of *being in a job/career that feels as if it is a deadend...boring... and unfulfilling*. (If this doesn't apply to you, substitute a limiting pattern that describes your situation.)

As we have been doing with previous issues, let's start by including the Five Standard Limiting Patterns:

P: **Being** *in a job/career that feels as if it is a deadend...boring...and unfulfilling*

P: **Wanting** *to be in a job/career that feels as if it is a deadend...boring...and unfulfilling*

P: **Feeling unworthy** *of not being in a job/career that feels as if it is a deadend...boring...and unfulfilling*

P: **Not doing what it takes** *to have it be different*

P: **Telling myself that undesirable or awful things would happen if I did not** *have this result, i.e., if I had something other than a job/career that feels as if it is a deadend...boring...and unfulfilling (then identify what those things are and reframe those beliefs and fears)*

You know the next step. What are some additional limiting patterns that contribute to this stifling job situation? Some of them may include:

P: Being afraid to have a job in which I would feel more responsible
P: Believing/feeling that I do not have what it takes to handle a more challenging, creative, interesting job
P: Believing/feeling that my innate skills are inadequate
P: Believing/feeling that I am inadequate...that I don't measure up
P: Fearing that I will be found out
P: Believing/feeling that I am a phony, a fraud, an imposter...that who I truly am is less than, worse than, what people see
P: Believing/feeling that I must keep myself insignificant and not call much attention to myself

Of course, any of these patterns will make it difficult for you to be or feel available to do work that you love. After all, if you loved your work, you would probably be inspired to expand your expertise; if you did that, someone might notice you...might even acknowledge you for who you are. Then what would happen? Under the *rules for life* we have just identified, that could be scary. However, if you remove these patterns, who knows what might happen?

So, just now, I suggest you turn to pages 46-47 and reframe all of the patterns that have come up since the last time you reframed.

The career patterns we have identified here will get you started. You can continue this process on your own.

Health Issues

Another potent area in which to apply *Essence Repatterning* is with health issues. It is a logical extension, especially since the medical profession now has validated, through scientific research, the connection between our health and our thinking patterns.

I have found that as limiting patterns are removed, individuals generally experience a heightened sense of well-being and often report the cessation of some physical symptoms—even when the patterns removed did not specifically address those symptoms. It appears that the body/mind sometimes uses physical symptoms as a vehicle for playing out specific *rules for life*.

Constricting Patterns

It has been exciting discovering the various physical changes that occur when *Essence Repatterning* is applied to some *rules for life*. One example of this is Karen, a woman in her '40s who had polio as a young child. Although her general health was good when she came for her first *Essence Repatterning* session, her post-polio symptoms included an atrophied lung and what she termed "a diminished ability to move air" through her chest. Consequently, she had been experiencing chronic breathing difficulties for many years.

Although we never specifically addressed Karen's difficulty in breathing as a limiting pattern during that session, we did work on issues of her *believing that she had to feel constricted, confined, and held back*. As we identified and removed various layers and permutations of these patterns and many others, we also dealt with those involving *low self-esteem* and f*eeling disempowered* and *out-of-control*.

At the beginning of Karen's second session, she reported that, since the last one, she had more physical energy and was acting more assertively. She reported speaking out with new confidence at a conference and even taking the position of devil's advocate. "This is something I don't usually do," she said. "In the past, I often would see something that should be brought up, but I didn't have the courage to say it."

In a session about a month later in early December, Karen casually mentioned that "I can now feel oxygen in my chest cavity even when I have a cold—and that is different." In that session she also told me that she had always had frequent colds during the winter, to the point that she was chronically sick an average of seven days a month.

Immune System

As we worked that day, I learned that Karen had a limiting pattern of *having an immune system that was not operating at peak capacity*—and also a pattern of *believing that it shouldn't operate at peak capacity*, as a *rule for life*.

As the limiting patterns emerged, we put on-line the pattern of Karen's *susceptibility to colds and flu*, and also her *belief that she had to mimic her mother's health* . (Her mother had had a disease related to calcification of the lungs and died at age 34 of complications arising from a cold.)

Karen's mother had been chronically ill from Karen's earliest memory. In fact, we discovered that Karen had a limiting pattern of *believing that it* was *necessary to have poor health in order to be part of her family.* We also found a *belief that she must manifest poor health* as a *rule for life.* In other words, in order to survive, i.e., play by the *rules for life*, she had to be sickly. (As we muscle-tested her body, we learned that the repeated bouts of pneumonia she began experiencing at age 23 were one of the ways this pattern played out.)

When we met three weeks later, the first changes she reported were, "I feel very empowered; the change is like night and day." As she looked back over her earlier emotional landscape, she recalled that she had felt "totally beaten down and sad...as if I had no control over what was happening to me."

"Now I have lots of ideas and want to get on with my life."

Part of the change she reported was a shift in her relationship with her husband. In earlier sessions we had identified and removed many limiting patterns connected to a general sense of feeling powerless and abused by the men in her family. We also had put on-line some of the dysfunctional family patterns that had been a part of her childhood.

When we met a month later, in late January, she reported that she had not missed any work time because of illness during December. This was a significant change from her previous, long-term experience of being sick one week a month during the winter. During an intense flu season in January (when people were typically out of work 10 days with the flu), she had it for only two days. "When I got it, I rebounded fast." She had gone from believing that being sickly was a *rule for life* to casually adding, "I didn't want it to bother me too much."

In early December, before we removed the limiting pattern of *having an immune system that was not operating at peak capacity*, I muscle-tested Karen to establish a rough benchmark of the degree to which her immune system *was* operating at peak capacity. I did this because I wanted to have a way to gauge any changes that might occur, so that we could track her progress.

Using a scale of 1 to 100, with 100 representing peak capacity and 1 representing least capacity, at that time her body/spirit indicated that her immune system was operating at 13 percent of peak capacity.

When I asked the same question in mid-March, it had increased to 85 percent of peak capacity.

The ways to apply *Essence Repatterning* to health issues are as varied as the health issues that may arise. While one may or may not always see an immediate outer manifestation of the removal of limiting patterns related to the issue, by removing some of the *need* for that symptom (as Karen did) it may be easier to improve one's overall health. One way this can manifest is that the repatterner may find himself drawn to the next healing approach that can assist him. This could include a new medication, a new health regime or technique, or even a new health practitioner. Again, the process is one of identifying and removing the patterns, layer by layer.

Repatterning Health-Related Issues

The first place to start is by listing the pattern of *having* the particular symptom or symptoms, whether they are physical, emotional, or mental. Next, apply the Five Standard Limiting Patterns—as demonstrated earlier in this chapter in the areas of money, relationships, and career.

Then, if you want to do a thorough job of it, apply those same Standard Limiting Patterns to every related pattern that you identify, based on the suggestions that follow.

Notice—and list as limiting patterns—how this symptom or condition makes you feel emotionally...the impact it has on your life...the restrictions or limitations it creates for you. What does this malady or condition say about you? What judgments or criticism do you place on yourself for having this condition? What does this condition *do* for you, what do you *get* by having this condition? (In other words, is there a distorted benefit you receive from having this condition?)

Next, you might notice any impact this symptom has on those around you. Is it is a bother or inconvenience to them, or do they show you extra attention as a result of it?

Then you might notice any way in which this symptom affects your relationships with others, and with yourself. Be sure to include any negative names you may have been called, or that you have called yourself, that may be related to your health or general self-esteem.

As you identify, list, and remove these limiting patterns, it will be important to notice and claim any changes you see in your emotional, mental—and physical—well-being.

To take this a step further, if you have an illness or condition that is thought to relate to specific emotional/mental patterns, use *Essence Repatterning* to remove those particular patterns as well. For example, asthma is often considered to be related to the emotional patterns of *feeling smothered and stifled*... and *being unable to breathe for one's self.*

SPECIFIC APPLICATIONS

For cancer, Louise Hay in *You Can Heal Your Life* cites what she calls the probable cause as patterns of *feeling deep hurt and longstanding resentment*...also that of *deep grief eating away at the self*...and *ongoing hatreds* and *feelings of futility*. (Her book, and others, offer information on the emotional/mental components related to many health conditions.)

Be as creative and inventive as you want in identifying the ways Ess*ence Repatterning* can help you with health-related issues. To give an idea of the range of applications, some of those who have used it successfully are people who have been allergic to cigarette smoke, bothered by pre-menstrual symptoms (PMS), been long-term smokers and chronically overweight.

Smoke Allergy

In the case of smoke allergy, Janice, the long-distance commuter mentioned earlier, reframed not only the physical symptoms she experienced when in an environment of cigarette smoking (which were most acute when she visited her parents because her mother smoked constantly), but also the emotional/mental components of the problem.

As she removed layer upon layer of limiting patterns in her life in general, she discovered patterns of *having to feel alienated*, and *feel bothered, by the world...separate, different*, and *generally out-of-sorts* and *ill at ease with her physical surroundings*. She discovered that all of this served to help her play out *rules for life* of having to *feel on-edge, insecure, threatened, and unsafe*.

As she removed these patterns, she found still others related to each of those adjectives and removed them as well. As a result, although she does not seek out smoke-filled rooms, she can go through entire weekends in her parents' small apartment and not be bothered by smoke. (She now says, "I don't even notice it.")

> Furthermore, she is more at ease with herself in general, more confident, and participating in her life in ways that are dramatically different from how it used to be just a few months ago.

Pre-Menstrual Syndrome

Often I have found that physical symptoms also reflect a need to keep one's self feeling impaired or disabled. This was the case with Brenda, a bubbly professional woman in her 30s, who found that her PMS discomfort was greatly diminished when she identified and removed, first, the emotional aspects of it and, second, the underlying patterns that demanded that she *periodically be irritable and hard-to-get-along-with*—just as her mother was.

Other components of the shift appear to be related to her removal of patterns that contributed to her *being and feeling confused, uncertain,* and *out of control.* Other patterns that may have an impact on PMS include those related to *rejecting one's femininity* or *womanhood* and *having to feel helpless and victimized.*

Smoking and Weight Issues

> As I mentioned earlier, physical imbalances often begin to right themselves as individuals work with general issues around self-esteem, fear of being seen, accepting one's self, and claiming one's power. This was the experience of Sylvia, a lovely, creative woman in her 40s, whose negative self-talk, cited earlier, was at odds with how naturally attractive she was. She began her first *Essence Repatterning* session by citing 1) her distrust of people, especially men, and 2) many behaviors or situations for which she was judging herself—including her lack of money, a car, and a big house...being misunderstood...forgetting her brother's graduation... smoking (for 20 years)...and being overweight.

As we worked together, we quickly found a meta-pattern of *having to do all the wrong things...and feel wrong and disempowered*. Since it was a meta-pattern, this meant that *having to do all the wrong things* (and *all* of the myriad of patterns which comprised this meta-pattern) was a pattern that pervaded her whole life, every breath.

As we explored this meta-pattern, she was able to see that, of course, she *had* to be judging herself, and *doing* things for which she could judge herself. After all, she *had to feel wrong* and *do wrong*, in order to survive (according to her particular *rules for life* and the resulting belief system).

Obviously, it could have been worse. When you consider the extremes of how the meta-pattern—of *having to do all the wrong things*—might have manifested, Sylvia was playing it out in relatively graceful ways...*and* they were holding her back.

A week after removing these patterns, Sylvia told me matter-of-factly by phone, "I've stopped smoking. I'm not even thinking about it."

Furthermore, she added, "I'm not eating as much, and I'm not feeling any urge to snack during the day." She said that how she felt about herself and others had changed, too. "I notice that people are being kinder to me, and also my concentration is better."

Metabolism Patterns

But weight issues, as with other common physical, behavioral issues, can manifest in many different ways. Brad, a successful financial analyst in his 40s, is an example of someone who could trace some of his weight-related patterns back to his relationship with his mother.

Although Brad had attained a significant degree of success in his own business, he did not feel successful with regard to relationships or his weight. When I met him, he was known for keeping himself very busy with work and writing his first book.

In his initial *Essence Repatterning* session, the patterns that quickly emerged included those of *believing he did not measure up...that he was fatally flawed...*and *that he had no right to be too successful.* As I muscle-tested him, we learned that all of these patterns were part of a meta-pattern of *having to impede his success...keep it at bay* and *feel disempowered and unsuccessful.*

In exploring the ramifications of this meta-pattern he acknowledged that he had made achieving the trappings of success his priority and put his relationship with himself last. This, along with a fear of intimacy—with himself and others—was creating an adversarial relationship with his body.

When he left the session, after removing these and many other patterns, he was no longer feeling insecure regarding his finances, weight, or relationships. (This did not mean that he had handled *all* of these issues, but that he had handled the top layer of them.)

When he returned three weeks later, I asked him what he had noticed that was different in his life since our last session. He had an immediate response: "Lately, I'm basically happy," he said. "I feel secure in myself...as if I could lose everything and know I'd be o.k." Also, he added, "Women are coming into my life."

In that session, he worked with a meta-pattern of *having to keep an agreement with his mother not to let anyone usurp her place.*

This meta-pattern was a total surprise to him (as was the previous meta-pattern.) He was not conscious of having made any such agreement with his mother; however, this meta-pattern checked out every step of the way as we identified some of the limiting patterns that comprised it.

(**Note:** In my work, I have found several men and women who have had limiting patterns related to some subconscious agreement they have made with one of their parents. While the nature of these agreements has been varied, there are some that have appeared more often than others. Many times, as in Brad's case, it is an agreement that makes it difficult to have fulfilling intimate relationships. Another fairly common one is an agreement that the child will *not overshadow* the parent. Needless to say, this kind of agreement can produce patterns of *having to stifle oneself...keep oneself small...*and even *keep oneself as a child.*)

For Brad, *having to keep this agreement with his mother* meant that he *had to be restrained and unfulfilled in his primary relationships.* He managed to do this by playing out patterns of *being attracted to the wrong kinds of women* and generally *keeping himself unfulfilled sexually, socially, and romantically.*

The additional patterns of *being overweight,* and *under-exercised,* clearly contributed to *keeping intimacy at bay* by helping him *feel insecure and inadequate.*

Although there were many emotional permutations to this meta-pattern, we also discovered a series of physical patterns that had a direct bearing on his weight. These were patterns of *having inadequate metabolism, assimilation and digestion.*

Again, in order to establish a rough benchmark against which to gauge any changes in his metabolism, before removing the patterns, I muscle-tested him to determine what his metabolism was (on a scale of 1 to 100, with 100 being optimal metabolism for him). The answer was 23 percent. Later, at the end of the session, after reframing all of the patterns mentioned, I asked the question again. This time the answer was 39 percent.

Not knowing what to expect, I looked forward to our next visit and checking his progress. When we met a month later, the first change he reported was that he was being *nicer* to himself. "I'm also exercising a little more and saying 'No' to work more often."

He had also started dating someone who had called him just after our last session. "She's more of a 'couch potato' than I am," he said with some wonder. When I asked him about her, he was quick to point out that she was not the kind of woman he would have chosen previously. "She's more reserved, like me. But she's *not* in my field, and she's *not* writing a book either." After a moment, he added, "Mainly, she is not intimidating."

As we discussed this new development, he said that previously he had been attracted to women with whom he felt in competition. They were high-powered women...marathon runners... and also writing books of their own.

Then I asked him more about his mother. Sure enough, she was a highly accomplished woman in almost every area of her life. She was so accomplished, in fact, that he felt inadequate in comparison, and always felt at odds and ill at ease with her.

As we talked, and muscle-tested for limiting patterns, he began seeing that one way he had been playing out the previous meta-pattern—and avoiding intimacy—had been by being attracted to women who were like his mother, women who were threatening to him and with whom he could *not* feel close and at ease. As soon as he removed those patterns, he made room for the kind of woman with whom he *could* feel comfortable and safe to be himself.

After removing the patterns that emerged for him that day—which centered on a meta-pattern of *experiencing life as a battle...and having to be a fighter*—I muscle-tested him to see if there was any change in the degree to which his metabolism was operating at peak capacity. There was. It was at 64 percent, up from 39 percent a month earlier.

Now, four weeks later, Brad has increased his exercise workouts to three times a week and has begun making more of an effort to eat a low-fat diet. "I'm finding it easier to exercise," he says, "and I'm more serious about wanting to lose weight." All in all, he sounds more content and satisfied with his life. "I'm enjoying myself more, and I've been attracting to me exactly what I need in terms of people and learning opportunities."

Final Reframing...For This Chapter

Perhaps you have been listing some limiting patterns as you've been reading, or perhaps they have been going on-line as you thought of them. At any rate, I urge you—now—to reframe whatever limiting patterns are up for you by turning to pages 46-47 and following the format there.

To recap what you've been doing throughout this whole chapter...in making the choice to remove specific limiting patterns, you have directed your unconscious to *reframe* these patterns, which means you have directed it *to generate and begin utilizing new behaviors that are superior* to the old ones for providing the intended benefit.

Again, the intended benefit for each of these patterns was most likely survival—that is, you had learned to believe that behaving and feeling in these old limiting ways was *the natural order of things*, the *rules for life*.

Creating New Architecture

In reframing these patterns, you have automatically set a new direction within yourself, created new *inner* architecture for a new way of being. Of course, using this metaphor, there are probably still other old neighborhoods to work with at another time, other limiting patterns to identify and remove. Most of us have many years, and decades, of living out these old ways, these old *rules for life*. Although there probably are some people who believe that they want to remove all of these *rules* in one fell swoop (and I was one of them), I have found that we will be offered only those patterns that are appropriate to be removed at a pace that we can readily and healthily absorb.

For example, as I look back to six months ago, there were some things that I wanted to know or be available to then that, in hindsight, I can see I was not ready for. This was because there were additional limiting patterns which I needed to address that I was not even aware of at the time.

Making the Changes Conscious

In the next chapter we will discuss how to bring the new *inner* architecture you have manifested to your *conscious* awareness, as a way of re-educating the ego about what the new *rules* or ways of living are that you have created.

However, it is important to know that just by reframing the limiting patterns you have identified, **you already have set a new direction**...you already have generated and begun utilizing new behaviors that are *superior* to the old ones for providing the intended benefit—of survival. You have shifted at least some of your inner architecture out of a surviving mode into more of a thriving mode.

Important

The *essential* aspect of *Essence Repatterning* is: identifying limiting patterns and reframing them. It is *not necessary* to do any more than continue identifying each next layer of limiting patterns and reframing them. If you do decide to identify and work with a *core choice,* as explained in the next chapter, that will be useful and valuable, but it is *not essential* to the process. The same is true if you decide then to work with *short-term* choices, or *pivotal* choices. If you are feeling overwhelmed, resistant, or short on time and/or energy, my recommendation is, first, that you reframe *these* patterns of feeling overwhelmed, resistant, etc., and, second, that you apply your time and energy to the fundamental task of identifying and removing the various layers of limiting patterns. *Then,* when you are naturally drawn to this chapter, *or* drawn to identifying *how* you want your life to be, you will be ready for the material in this chapter.

7

Setting a New Conscious Direction

This chapter discusses:
1) Various kinds of choices ;
2) How to fully align with your choices;
3) How to have a clear track to receive what you've chosen; and
4) How to use your choices to highlight those patterns that are blocking you.

Once you have reframed a major series of patterns, you may find yourself automatically thinking about how you would like your life to be now. This chapter will focus on how you can most effectively set a new, *conscious* direction that will help you re-educate your ego in the new values by which you want to be guided (in place of those old *rules*).

This chapter will begin with a discussion of long-term, core choices and short-term, supplemental choices. You will learn how to word your choices in ways that will make them more powerful. You also will learn how to align with them, and to clear the track to receive these new results and ways of being. In addition, you will learn how to work daily with choices and how to use them to discover which limiting patterns are preventing you from having what you desire.

New Architecture

Every time you reframe even one limiting pattern, you are creating new architecture, new pathways *within* you that will allow you to be different, to be healthier, and to live and act from more of the *essential* you...yes, from your *essence*. **It is not necessary to do anything more to set that new inner direction.** By identifying each specific limiting pattern—and reframing it—you are doing that automatically.

(Of course, once you've reframed those patterns, you will see the next layer that is ripe for reframing, but it is important to know that you have already set a new inner direction for the particular patterns you've reframed...and nothing more is required.)

However, after you have reframed a major series of limiting patterns, if you find yourself thinking of how you want to *be*, or how you want your life to be, now that those old patterns are gone, your *essence* may be suggesting that you make this new inner direction apparent to your *conscious* awareness. By doing this you will be re-educating your ego in the new inner directions you have set for yourself through the reframing process.

Core Choice

The most effective way to direct your consciousness—and ego—is through the use of *choice*. The choice that emerges after a lengthy *Essence Repatterning* session usually will be what I call a core choice, one that will have a broad, all-encompassing impact on all aspects of your life.

Many people spend their lives wanting, wishing, or hoping for what they desire. These are all relatively passive approaches. The direct approach for moving our consciousness toward what we want is through *choosing* the result we desire.

The limiting patterns you have removed came out of old *rules for life* that are physiologically stored in the back part of our brain where all our history is held. That is where the ego holds sway, drawing on how things *have been* in the past as the criteria for how things *should be* in the future.

However, when you *choose* a particular result or direction, and actually say the words *I choose*, followed by the result you want, you naturally move your energy out of a primary focus in the back part of the brain and activate the forebrain.

In working with Three-In-One Concepts, which originally was developed to assist those with dyslexic learning disabilities, I learned that the forebrain is the *newest* part of the brain in terms of evolution, where *possibilities not yet experienced* originate. The forebrain is physically located behind your forehead, in the area of the pineal gland, or what some call the third eye.

When we activate the forebrain, we are opening ourselves to create unfulfilled desires which, until now, have been relegated to the category of hopes and dreams within us.

Putting Choice Into Action

To put this information into action, briefly review the patterns, the *rules* for life, you have removed. These were the old ways of being. If you could set a new direction for how you'd like to live your life, what are the words or phrases that come to mind? As best you can, allow yourself to sense these from that new place you've created within you, from that new architecture.

Write these words and phrases down.

For example, if you hear or sense that you want to *feel worthy and that you are enough,* and also to *feel confident,* these words may be the core of the new values by which you want to be living your life.

The way to word this as a choice would be:

I choose to feel worthy, enough and confident— and know it.

Automatic Feedback Loop

By adding the words *and know it,* you are automatically building in a feedback loop that will allow you—and your ego—to claim these changes as they occur. You probably know people who have made significant changes, but they are the last to know, or claim it. This can be the ego's resistance to change.

Go *Toward* What You Want

By the way, in formulating your choice, it is important to word it in such a way that it supports you in going *toward* what you want, instead of *away* from what you don't want. For example, choosing to *feel worthy and confident* is going toward what you want. If you were to choose to *not feel bad about yourself* or to *not be afraid,* you would be trying to go away from what you don't want.

Similarly, in making choices regarding financial issues, it will not be supportive to include, and therefore be focusing on, words such as *poor, lack,* or *not enough.*

(A tip: any time you include the word *not,* or words beginning with *un-*, as in unafraid or unconfident, you are probably going *away* from what you don't want, instead of *toward* what you do want.)

Activating the Limbic Part of the Brain

As an experiment, I'd like you to add another word to the choice you are working with, or if you haven't formulated one yet, to the one we're using in the example above. First of all, read this choice, or say it out loud as it's been originally presented:

> *I choose to feel worthy, enough and confident—and know it.*

Now try saying it with the addition of the word *enjoy:*

> *I choose to **enjoy** feeling worthy, enough and confident—and know it.*

Do you notice a difference? Most people find that by adding the word *enjoy,* it makes whatever they are choosing lighter or more fun.

At the same time, it's actually a technical addition. By including the word *enjoy*, you are activating the limbic part of the brain, a part of the brain that's closely connected to the emotions. By including this emotional component, you automatically give yourself more inner support for having the result you are choosing.

Another way to activate the limbic system in your choices is to word them in such a way that you are choosing *to feel good* about a relationship or situation, or even *to feel great* about it.

For example, if what you want is *to be true to yourself* and *trusting your deepest knowing* (concepts which could emerge after you have done an in-depth session of *Essence Repatterning*), you might word your choice:

> *I choose to feel good (or great) about how true to myself I am being and how much I am trusting my deepest knowing—and know it.*

This choice then will lead you naturally to the kinds of decisions and behaviors that will allow you to feel good or great about how true to yourself you are being and how much you are trusting your deepest knowing.

Note: This choice is n*ot* about having you feeling good/great about your *current* state of being true to yourself, etc. You are *not* feeling good about it—or as good as you want to feel about it—or you would not be making a choice about it. This choice *will* lead you to a level of behavior of being true to yourself, etc., that you *can* feel good or great about.

Choose the *Experience* You Want

As you look at the core choice you have made as a result of repatterning, you will notice that it is probably a rather fundamental choice that is not keyed to a specific, finite outcome in your life, such as exercising three times a week, losing 10 pounds, or having a wonderful relationship.

The choice we have been working with...*I choose to enjoy feeling worthy, enough and confident—and know it*...is an example of this. In this choice, you are *not* choosing the *circumstances*; you *are* choosing the *experience* that you want. By working with a choice that is broader and more encompassing, you are ensuring that you don't limit how the result shows up. If you did, it could only be based upon what you have experienced in the past...for that is all your conscious mind knows.

Choose the *What*— and the *How* Will Show Up

When we choose *what* we want—the experience we are looking for—then the *how to* automatically shows up in the fullest sense for which we are ready. By not trying to pin down *how* it shows up, we give our Spirit, the unconscious, or the universe (whichever words work for you), the most freedom to create the fullest experience of which we are capable at this time.

Remember, by working with choice, actually saying the words *I choose*, you are activating the part of the brain where *possibilities not yet experienced* originate. In these more fundamental, all-encompassing core choices that we're discussing, any attempt to control the way they play out will, by necessity, be dictated by what we *think* is possible. What we think is possible is dictated by what we have experienced in the past, i.e., by what is stored in our back brain.

Of course it is the ego that likes to know and determine how things are going to play out, as a means of trying to be in control. When we leave it to the ego to make these determinations, the only criteria it has to use for determining *future* results are *past* results, results that will be in accordance with those old *rules for life*.

However, by freely choosing the quality of life you want—how you want to be *experiencing* your life—you are moving yourself *toward* these new ways of being and experiencing life...without knowing *how* that is going to play out. This is part of the adventure of watching your life unfold in new, more fulfilling and enriching ways.

Short-term Choices

Once you have identified your core choice, that may be all you need to work with at this time. However, perhaps there are specific, material results that you want. In this case some short-term, finite choices may seem to emerge naturally from your core choice. In the case of short-term results, you are consciously identifying specific results you want in the relatively short term. This time span could be anywhere from the next few days up to several months.

> One example of this occurred in my work with Shiela, a workaholic lawyer in a small law firm she helped start. She came to the session in crisis over her finances and the conflict she was experiencing with her partners and how they were treating her. Furthermore, she had a meeting with them scheduled for later that day, one that she had been putting off until she felt she could handle it emotionally and have all the data she needed in order to be fully prepared.
>
> During that session, we focused on many limiting patterns that arose from two meta-patterns (patterns that pervade her whole life): the pattern of *having to be on edge* and the pattern of *walking on eggshells.*
>
> Given her childhood with an alcoholic, workaholic father, these patterns were not surprising, since she and her siblings lived in a household that was generally on edge and mincing around both dad's mood-swings and his demanding standards. During the session we explored how these meta-patterns specifically were reflected in her work, relationship with money, and intimate relationships.
>
> After identifying and repatterning all of the manifestations of these meta-patterns that she was ready to do that day, the choice that emerged for her was:
>
> > *I choose to enjoy freely creating a playful life I desire—and know it.*
>
> (Sometimes the choice that emerges after a major repat-

terning session may be surprising. In Shiela's case, she had removed many patterns that related to *life being a struggle and hard*, and *feeling anxious* and *stressful*—which were some of the ways she experienced life as a child. Notice that the choice that emerged from her new *inner* architecture—which, in effect, gives her permission to freely create the kind of playful life *she* wants—is just the opposite of those old patterns.)

While she could feel the rightness of this core choice for her, she also wanted, in view of the pivotal meeting she had that afternoon, to formulate a choice that would relate directly to that and other decisions concerning whether or not to continue in business with her partners. The short-term choice that emerged to address these issues was:

> I choose to feel great about the success of my business, my peace around it, and all the decisions surrounding it—and know it.

In other words, she was choosing to a) have her business *be* so successful... b) have herself *feel* so peaceful... and c) to be making the *quality* of decisions—that she could feel great about.

Shiela left the session feeling calm, empowered, and with a "let's see what happens" attitude. When I spoke with her a couple days later, she reported with some awe in her voice that the meeting had gone better than she could have imagined. "Everyone was peaceful and caring. It was a complete turnaround."

When I spoke to her three weeks later, she was enthusiastic about just having acquired a second new client that month. She also mentioned that she was close to being on-target with her business goals. Now, months later, she is happily out of that difficult business partnership *and* enjoying good relations with her former partners.

While the short-term choice Shiela made was right for her, it could also have been worded other ways as well. Another approach she could have taken regarding that business meeting is: *I choose to have an outcome that I feel great about—and know it*...or... *I choose to enjoy having an empowering, successful relationship with my business partners—and know it*...or...*I choose to feel great about my finances, business relationships, and personal success—and know it.*

Setting Yourself Up to Win

By choosing the *experience* that you want, whatever the *outcome* involved, you generally are setting it up to win. When you don't include the *quality* of result that you want, you may be surprised at the outcome. Although I've talked about this with regard to core choices, it is equally as important with short-term choices.

One simple example of this can be seen in the area of relationships. I have worked with individuals who so desperately wanted a primary relationship that their choice was very simple: *I choose to have a relationship.*

If you are currently in a relationship, or ever have been, you probably know that it is possible to have wonderful relationships, loving ones, terrible ones, even very unfulfilling ones. If you simply choose *to have a relationship*, you may be leaving yourself wide open to any kind of relationship—probably the kind you have experienced in the past, or what you saw growing up. So when someone tells me they *choose to have a relationship*, I ask: "Would you like it to be a good one?" Of course, they say, "Yes;" but I stress that "I wouldn't take that result for granted with your choice as you have stated it."

Relationship Choices

Clearly, in working with relationship issues, it can be essential to include the experience you are looking for in wording your choice. For example, you might choose...*to enjoy having a wonderful relationship with a man/woman—and know it…or…to have a primary relationship I feel great about—and know it…or…to enjoy having a primary relationship that is more wonderful than I could imagine—and know it.*

This last choice can be effective if you have been trying to list every quality that you want in your relationship, or partner, but are afraid you will leave something crucial out. For example, what if you include such qualities as loving, caring, supportive, fulfilling, playful, etc., but omit others that may also be important to you, such as healthy, clean, abundant, respectful, faithful, etc.?

The point is that if you choose both a) the way you want to *experience* and *feel* about a result, and b) the result itself, then you have the best chance to create a result that pleases you.

Just as identifying limiting patterns is always a step-by-step process, so is making effective choices. As you experiment with this, be patient with yourself. I have found that learning how to effectively direct these inner parts of ourselves is a skill that is continually evolving. Because these inner parts can be very literal in terms of how choices are worded, you might work with one choice, and then notice that what is coming to you is not exactly what you wanted. There have been times when, dismayed with the result that has shown up, I have heard myself incredulously say outloud: "I chose this?!"

Yes, I did, based upon 1) the way I worded my choice, and 2) the *rules for life* under which I was operating at the time. When things show up that we don't like, or don't quite fit the picture we *now* realize that we had in mind, these are simply limiting patterns which we can reframe. Also, this feedback provides valuable information that can help us word our choice more effectively.

Avoid Manipulative Choices

How we word our choices can be important for another reason as well. Going back to Shiela and her business, you will notice that her choice was *not* about how others would behave, but always about her own behavior or feelings, how *she* wanted to feel about her business success, peace of mind, and decisions. This is crucial to the process—and this is where our real power of choice lies: in choosing how we, ourselves, want to behave, be, or feel.

If Shiela had chosen for her partners to behave a certain way, she would have been manipulative and invasive of them. Manipulation destroys relationship. Furthermore, the choice process breaks down when we use it to manipulate others. If we use it to try and control others, we may find ourselves getting diminished results even for the choices that don't involve others.

The key here is to make choices about the experience that *we* want to have—and not give the power for the success of our choice to forces outside ourselves. We can always choose to have results that we *will feel great—or good—about*. That way we don't limit how the results show up, either. Then, whatever kinds of results that we will feel great about will have a chance to show up, for *those* are the kinds of results we are choosing.

I have worked with individuals who were interviewing for particular jobs and who were tempted to choose to land a specific job with a specific company. My suggestion was that they go for the experience they want, rather than the specific job. This puts the power for their choice back inside them, instead of giving it to a particular personnel manager. Some examples of this are:

> *I choose to enjoy having a job, and salary, I love—and know it...or...I choose to feel great about my work, fulfillment, and salary—and know it....or... I choose to enjoy doing work I love and being paid well for it—and know it...or...I choose to enjoy feeling worthy, fulfilled, and well paid in my work—and know it.*

Choices That Involve Others

Although it is strongly suggested that you not make choices

about how others will behave, there is a way you can involve specific others in your choices—without being manipulative or invasive.

Years ago, one of my clients, Helen, a gracious, wealthy woman in her 60s, said, "Pat, I know I can't choose to have my husband make the right investment decisions, but I am not pleased with the way things are going. Is there any way I can deal with this in terms of choice?"

The answer was yes. If what she wants is for Douglas, her husband, to make investment decisions that she feels great about, she can choose that:

> *I choose to feel great about Douglas' investment decisions—and know it.*

This was the choice she made, with good results. It can work just as well with a boss who mistreats you: *I choose to feel great about how my boss treats* me—*and know it.* Then see how that plays out.

Choose the Result—Not the Process

As I learned from Robert Fritz, author of *The Path of Least Resistance*, when you choose the *result*, instead of the *process*, you make room for the unknowable to occur. For example, I would always choose *to have my bills paid off,* rather than choose *to pay them off!* In this case, the result I want is to be debt free, or to *have* my bills paid off—not to be paying them off. If I choose the latter—*to be paying off my bills*—I could be doing that indefinitely. If I choose *to have them paid off,* that is a finite result, not an ongoing process.

If the result I want is *to be debt-free,* I would choose that, rather than choose *to have the money to pay them off.* Choosing the former leaves room for the unexpected. I have known of people who have chosen to be debt-free and been very surprised at how that played out. (Choosing *to be financially free and clear* may be even better than choosing *to be debt-free,* since it does not focus on the debt at all.)

Notice that when we choose to have the money to do something, we are choosing the process, not the result. If you want to go on a fabulous vacation, choose *to have* a fabulous vacation, not *to have the money for* a vacation. Again, who knows how that vacation result might appear.

I know of a young woman who was financially strapped, but knew she desperately needed a vacation. By choosing to have a wonderful vacation, she made room for someone to offer her a speaking engagement in the Southwest and the wherewithal to finance the getaway she needed.

Money Choices

In applying some of these suggestions to choices about money, here are some examples that incorporate some of these principles: *I choose to feel great about my income—and know it*...or... *I choose to enjoy having ample money and resources to meet my wants and needs—and know it*...or, perhaps the best, because it includes action steps:...*I choose to enjoy knowing and doing exactly what it takes to have all the money I want and need—and know it.*

Notice that I have not suggested choosing to have a job that will give me all the money I want and need. Why? First, choosing to have the job, rather than the money itself, is only the process to the result. Second, what if you had an opportunity to go into a successful business of your own? Third, what if you opened to *passive* income—income you did not have to work for? Some obvious ways to generate passive income are through receiving interest on successful investments, royalties on books, franchise operations, having people sell your product or teach and market your courses—any way in which you do not actively work to earn the money yourself.

What if someone wanted to offer it to you, or you could become a silent partner in a successful business? What if you found an heirloom in the attic and sold it? The possibilities are extensive, and, again, I have seen and heard about some pretty remarkable ways that choices have played out when the choice is for the result, not the process.

Action Steps

One nice thing about choice is that knowing *what* you want is *most* important—*not* how to get it. Once you have put your choice fully in motion— using the techniques suggested in this chapter—then the particulars of how to achieve that result will show up. **This is especially true when you take even small action steps toward that result each day...*and when* you continue to identify and repattern any behavior, belief, treatment by others, and emotional/mental/spiritual issue that limits you.**

I can't emphasize enough the importance of taking *small* action steps toward the result you have chosen. Understand, you don't have to know the *perfect* next step to take, or even be invested in the result of that next step. What is important is that you *take* that next step, and then the one after that. By doing this, you give your creative parts the message that you are serious about having the result you've chosen.

When we stay focused *only* on the next, small step toward our chosen result, it is easier to stay present and not be overwhelmed by the challenges (or possibilities) of any of the other steps to be taken later.

I have found both in my own endeavors, and in coaching others, that there often can be a strong tendency to begin by *identifying* not just the first small step, but the next one, and then the one after that, and even the one after that—*before the first step has even been taken.* This is an easy way to sabotage ourselves.

When we have not yet established the foundation which is created by taking the first step, and each subsequent one, it can be overwhelming to be focusing on the fourth, fifth, or sixth step down the line. By focusing only on the step in front of us (and reframing any limiting pattern to do otherwise), we make it easier to build a successful foundation for the result we have chosen.

Moreover, practically speaking, until we have taken the first step and seen where that takes us, we really cannot know what the second step should be. For example, say you have decided to initiate a family reunion to take place next summer. Perhaps you have chosen *to enjoy having a family reunion you feel great about—and know it.*

One small next step could be to call your mother and bounce the idea off of her. Before you take that first step, however, you may find yourself thinking that the second step will be finding a location you really like.

But perhaps the place that pops into your mind is one which would require a substantial downpayment to hold the space. At this point you may find yourself thinking about how you could get that kind of money...and who in the family might chip in on it. This line of thought might remind you how hard it is to get along with one branch of the family...and then how difficult it will be to get consensus...etc.

By this time, the idea for a reunion may feel like a lot of work, overwhelming, and not worth the effort. How could it feel otherwise when you haven't even placed the first brick in the foundation for this chosen result by taking that first small step of calling your mother?

Who knows what the outcome of that conversation might be. Perhaps you will learn that someone else already has started the ball rolling and that you don't have to carry the load alone, psychologically or otherwise. Or perhaps your mother will mention it to another family member who suggests that the idea be discussed with an uncle who has a big farm which could host the reunion. This could mean that all your financial and emotional concerns have been unnecessary.

While this example has dealt with what could be a major project, working with action steps is very effective with small results as well.

When Greg, a middle-aged attorney, wanted to have his car washed, inside and out, he was smart enough not to choose to do it himself. Instead, he chose *to enjoy having a clean car.* By the time he had gone out to wash his car, he was surprised to find that a friend had vacuumed the interior of it for him.

I've even seen this happen with things such as housecleaning. When Gladys was learning how to make effective choices, she decided that she wanted to have her house cleaned, and assumed that meant she should choose to clean it. I suggested, however, that instead of choosing *to clean it,* or even choosing *to have cleaned it* (the result she *thought* she wanted—which assumed that she would have to do it herself)...that she choose *to enjoy having* a clean house, the *real* result she wanted.

The day after making this choice, a relative called to say she was coming to town unexpectedly. As it turned out, this was an aunt who always cleaned Gladys' home, every time she visited!

Using Gladys' experience as an example, these approaches can be applied to any project you want to have completed, at home or at work. You can also apply them to such results as: *feeling great about the success of the party I'm giving... enjoying myself Saturday night...having a fun afternoon with my kids...feeling great about a pending job interview.*

Aligning With Your Choice

Once you have made your choice(s), there is a simple way that you can give yourself even more inner support for this result. By choosing to be in alignment with your choice, you heighten the impetus toward the result you desire. When I muscle-test individuals before making this specific choice for alignment, and then afterwards, there is always a significant increase in inner support for having the result they have chosen.

The choice for alignment is:

I choose to enjoy being in full support of and alignment with this choice and result...
and with the choice to be receiving Optimal support for this from the Unconscious and other sources.

Since you are choosing and asking only for *optimal* support from the Unconscious and other sources, you are assured that you are opening *only* to positive input from your High Self, Spirit, God, Buddha, etc., whatever the Unconscious and *other sources* might include.

Having a Clear Track

By choosing to be in full support of and alignment with your choice and result, it is as if you are the engineer of a steam locomotive that has built up a full head of steam. Your hand is on the throttle and you are ready to deliberately pull it back into the On-position, and move forward toward what you've chosen.

At this point, I have learned, through much testing and experience, that there is still one additional step to take to give yourself the momentum that will propel you forward toward the result you desire.

What you have done thus far—in identifying the result you desire…choosing it…and aligning with it—has given you a clear green-light *inside* you for this result. However, I have learned to check if there is a *clear track* in front of you for you to *receive* this result…to *have* it…to *want* it…and to *feel worthy* of it.

I learned this particular part of the process the hard way, thinking I had done everything required to achieve a particular result, only to discover later that I had not had a clear track to receive it, have it, want it, and feel worthy of it.

In checking many, many people, in individual sessions and in seminar settings, I have found consistently at this point in the process that, for whatever reason, there is *not* a clear track to *receive* this result, to *have* it, to *want* it, and to *feel worthy* of it.

The good news is that this is simply a limiting pattern, and can be dealt with very easily.

In order to have a clear track to *receive* the result you have chosen, to *have* it, *want* it, and *feel worthy* of it, you simply reframe this pattern:

> P: **Not** *having a clear track to Receive this result, Have it, Want it, and Feel Worthy of it*

As you would with any limiting pattern, simply say:

I choose to reframe these patterns, and all allied limiting patterns, now and to know it.

Note: For this unique situation, it is *not* necessary to put on-line all of the permutations from pages 46-47 before reframing this pattern.

Once you have made a formal choice for a specific result you desire, you only have to make the choice *to be in alignment* with it once, and it is done. Also, you need only choose to reframe *not having a clear track*, etc., once for each choice.

Re-educating Your Ego— Making Your Choice a Reality

Whatever choice(s) you have made and begun working with represent the new values you are finding within you. In order to bring these values into your outer world of everyday physical reality, it is useful to re-educate your ego regularly and consistently about what these new values are.

Up until now, because of the countless mixed messages each of us has given ourselves at deep levels within our subconscious (based on our early programming and *rules for life*), we have not always seen positive results when we, at one time or another, consciously have said: "Now, I want to be moving in a new direction."

After all, why should any new proclamation be believed? What makes any new decision for ease, or clarity, or happiness, different from the random beliefs and wishes, hopes and dreams, we have dallied with through the decades?

One difference is that you now have the opportunity to use *Essence Repatterning* to create new inner directions for yourself. Another plus is that you also have the opportunity to begin working with choices in significant ways—aligning with your choice(s) and clearing the track to have those results.

The next step in this re-education process of the ego is to

make these choices a conscious part of your daily routine—simply by reading your *I choose...* statements at least twice a day, preferably each morning and night. (You also can say them throughout your day if you want to give your choices extra emphasis. Some people put it on a small card and keep it in their pocket or put it on their telephone, bathroom mirror, or the dashboard of their car.)

Every time you consciously choose *how* you want to be feeling or acting, or *what* you want to be experiencing, you are redirecting your ego out of the old limiting ways of being into the new ones you have consciously selected.

By doing this for at least a few weeks, you will be telling your ego that these decisions for change are unlike those old hopes and dreams, randomly made. You will be letting your ego know that you are serious about these new values and about making them an integral part of your life.

The Power of Choice

You've probably heard the adage: "Be careful what you ask for, you might get it."

People who work with choice know how important this is. As I mentioned earlier, *wanting* something is one thing; *choosing* it is another—especially when you do it in the ways that are being suggested here.

It is important to understand that whatever choice we make is more than just a conscious direction to have that result. By inference, it is also a request to consciously know and deal with whatever limiting patterns stand between us and having that result fully in our lives.

Parents and Bosses

For example, in one particular session with Louis, a lighthearted man in his 30s who is an administrator for a small marketing firm, the limiting patterns he addressed that day arose out of being and feeling emotionally abused and victimized by his mother and father.

Once he had reframed all of the patterns that were identified, and consequently set a new direction *within* him toward healthier ways of being, the choice that emerged out of this new, inner architecture was:

I choose to enjoy feeling respected, honored, appreciated, loved, and worthy—and to know it.

As we completed the session, I told him that whatever limiting patterns prevented him from fully living that choice would become evident. In other words, whatever limiting patterns precluded him from feeling respected and honored, etc., would surface to be addressed. Over the next few days and weeks, he found that, while the specific patterns of abuse and victimization that he had reframed were gone, other versions of them emerged. These played out most intensely in his relationship with his female supervisor.

In order to understand why this happens it is useful to know that while the specific old limiting patterns were reframed into what is now new *architecture* within him, there are other limiting patterns, metaphorically speaking, *other neighborhoods* of patterns, that have not yet been addressed. Although the limiting ego has lost some of its power to run the show—specifically in terms of the patterns that were removed in that session—these *old neighborhoods* represent other old *rules of life* that the ego can draw on to try and maintain its control.

Since Louis' ego had less power in the new architecture within him, it was forced to seek out some of the old neighborhoods where it was still king, where it could still run the show. So although Louis was choosing to feel respected and honored, etc., and had created more room to receive that, the limiting ego began using other limiting patterns to inhibit him from fully experiencing that respect and honoring.

The good news is that as the ego began doing this, it was simply showing Louis the next layer of limiting patterns to be identified and removed.

More Grist For the Mill

Now, months later, Louis has learned to do *Essence Repatterning* for himself and has begun treating every glitch, every disagreement, every mistreatment, as just more grist for the mill, more raw material to reframe.

As a result, his work life has improved in unexpected ways. "My boss is treating me better," he says. "She is giving me choices about scheduling my time in ways she has never done before. Before this, she had always decided what would work for her and left it to me to work around her schedule."

Furthermore, because of staff cutbacks and belt-tightening in this little company, he hadn't expected to be able to take any vacation this year. To his surprise, his boss has suggested that he do so—and at the time he always has chosen in the past. "She even has urged me to take some time off by leaving early on Friday afternoons this summer."

Louis has made some significant shifts in terms of his relationship with his parents as well. One of these shifts centers on family visits. "For years I have been making obligatory trips home almost every holiday," he says. "Now I have decided that I want to spend that time with my friends." Instead of acting out of guilt and obligation, he now goes to visit his parents at other times, when it better suits *his* schedule.

Business Applications

Another example of the power of choice are the results manifested by Larry Sagen, director of the International Youth Hall of Fame in Seattle. His goal is to shift the culture's prevailing paradigm from *youth as problems* to *youth as resources.*

Two years ago Larry left his business to start this non-profit organization, which is aimed at mobilizing communities, businesses, schools, media, government officials, parents, and youth to work together to recognize and support the positive contributions of young people.

Although his long-range vision was clear, he says: "The implementation has been a challenge beyond belief." Even though he had a business plan and knew he needed committed volunteers, money, an office, computers and office equipment, he says, "My past strategies and tactics just weren't getting me to those goals."

He adds that there were many convenient excuses for all of this: the economy, for one, and the existing funding commitments cited by foundations, businesses, and individual contributors. "My frustration level increased daily. I was stuck."

Moving Past Resistance

However, in November, 1991, he says all of that changed. "That's when I began working with this particular process of choice. It has helped me get through my resistance to succeed."

After using the process for less than nine months, he reports that: Apple Computers has donated two computers and a laser printer to his organization; a Seattle bank has donated a 600-square-foot office in a prestigious building on Seattle's waterfront; and the mayor of Tacoma, Washington, has committed to creating the Tacoma Youth Hall of Fame Recognition Program and a permanent exhibit designed by Tacoma youth. As part of this major shift in momentum, Larry says,

"Volunteers are calling me to help with the Tacoma program, an art auction, a Youth History program, and day-to-day operations."

Based on these results, he says, "I continue to use the process and update my choices each week." (Larry is so thorough that he has made laminated copies of his choices, one of which he keeps next to his desk. Another is on his closet mirror, and the third hangs in his shower!)

Choice vs. Affirmations

Since we are talking about the power of choice in this section, let's discuss affirmations as well. If you have ever used affirmations (i.e., "I *am* enjoying financial abundance and prosperity" or "I *am* relaxed and at peace with myself"), you may be wondering how *choosing* the result you desire compares with *affirming* that you already have it.

One difference is that people who have tried it both ways consistently report that the results they *choose* manifest much faster.

Another difference is that when we *choose* a result, we are *directing* our consciousness and energy *toward* the result that we want. When we *affirm* a result that we want, actually *telling ourselves we already have it* (as in "I *am* relaxed and at peace..."), we are giving ourselves a contradictory message and telling ourselves something that is not true. Otherwise, why would we be affirming it in the first place?

These contradictory messages can backfire on us in other ways, too. Considering all the mixed messages we have given ourselves through the years, it's no wonder that so many of us don't have what we say we want. For instance, take the woman who *says* that she really wants a loving relationship—and perhaps even is choosing it, using the approaches suggested here. Then, in the next breath, you hear her complain, "But all the good men are gone;"... "Relationships have never worked for me;"... "Men are no good anyway; it's not safe to let them get too close." It's no wonder she doesn't have the relationship she desires, given the messages she has stored in her subconscious.

If you notice yourself articulating these kinds of negative thoughts, either to yourself or outloud to others, you would be ahead of the game to notice that they represent limiting beliefs and use *Essence Repatterning* to reframe them. Obviously, the more of these negative, contradictory messages you can remove from the subconscious, the easier it will be to achieve the results you desire.

Key Components of Choice

1. **Choose what you want, rather than what you don't want.**
   (Ex: *I choose to be enjoy being happy—and know it*...rather than *I choose to enjoy not being sad and unhappy, etc.*)

2. **Choose the experience that you want, rather than the circumstances.**
   (Ex: *I choose to enjoy having a job that I love—and know it*...rather than: *I choose to enjoy being marketing director of ABC Corp., etc.* By working with *Essence Repatterning* and making choices in these powerful ways, you may find that the work you presently are doing, or thought you *should be* doing, is not what you *want* to be doing. Most individuals who use this process naturally find themselves gravitating toward the kind of work, and experiences, that are more aligned with their *essential* Self.)

3. **Provide your ego with an automatic feedback loop that will help it notice that your choice is working...simply by adding the words—*and know it*—to every choice.**

4. **Create more emotional support for your choice by activating the limbic part of the brain...by simply including the words *enjoy* or *feel good* (or *great*) *about* whatever result you are choosing.**
   (Ex: *I choose to receive a raise I feel great about—and know it*...or: *I choose to enjoy receiving a raise that is better than I could have imagined—and know it*...instead of simply: *I choose to get a raise—and know it.*)

5. **Choose the *quality* of result that you want, rather than just the result.**
   (Ex: *I choose to enjoy having a new home that I love—and know it*...rather than just: *I choose to enjoy having a new home—and know it.* By choosing the *quality* of home that you want, you increase your chances of *not* ending up with a home with bad plumbing, sagging foundations, termites, etc., because you probably wouldn't love that kind of home.)

6. Avoid manipulative choices—choose the experience that *you* want to have...rather than choosing how *someone else* should act or perform.
   (Ex: I *choose to feel good about my relationship with Karen—and know it*...rather than: *I choose to have Karen treat me fairly, etc.*...or: *I choose to feel great about the financial settlement with my ex-husband—and know it*...rather than: *I choose to enjoy having my ex-husband give me a settlement that is exactly what I want, etc.*)

7. Choose the *true result* you want—*without* limiting the process of how that result may manifest!
   (Ex: *I choose to enjoy having a new car I love—and know it*...rather than: *I choose to enjoy buying a new car, etc.* In this case, *buying* the car is process. What you *want* is a new car you love.)

8. Identify one *small* action step you could take toward having the result you've chosen...then take it. Continue doing this, step by step, focusing *only*, repeat, *only*, on the small, *next* step that is right in front of you.
   (Ex: If you have made the choice *to enjoy having a successful, fulfilling business of your own—and know it*... then identify one *small, next* step you could take toward that result. Perhaps it would be calling your Uncle John who has the kind of business you've considered going into. Perhaps it is going to the library to do some research...or getting your finances straightened out so you know exactly how much money you have to start with, or how much you would need each month to tide yourself over during a business start-up period.)

9. Align with your choice...to receive optimal inner and outer support for the result you have chosen. Once you have identified and written down your choice(s), make this choice:
   I choose to enjoy being in full support of and alignment with this choice and result...
   and with the choice to be receiving Optimal support for this from the Unconscious and other sources.

10. Clear the track...to *receive* the result you have chosen, to *have* it, *want* it, and *feel worthy* of it, by simply reframing this pattern:

> P: **Not** *having a clear track to Receive this result, Have it, Want it, and Feel Worthy of it.*

—Do this by saying:

> *I choose to reframe these patterns, and all allied limiting patterns, now and to know it.*

11. Re-educate your ego regarding the new values and ways of life you have chosen...by saying your choice(s) each morning and night.

Starting With Your Choice

The first part of this chapter has dealt primarily with two basic contexts of choice:

1. The *core* choice that might emerge from an extended session of Basic *Essence Repatterning*; and
2. How to *make* short-term choices...how to *word* them... and how to *work* with them.

When you identify a core choice that seems to almost naturally emerge at the end of a substantial session of *Essence Repatterning*, that choice is coming out of the new inner architecture you have created through the repatterning process. In other words, *it is a product of the reframing you have done.*

When you identify choices at other times—choices that have not emerged after a concentrated session of E*ssence Repatterning*—they are coming out of your specific desire to have you, or your life, be different. These choices are emerging out of your *thoughts* or *feelings—not* necessarily out of new architecture you have created through reframing. These choices are just as valid as the core ones that emerge from a repatterning session. In fact, by identifying these choices, you are showing yourself the next level of reframing you are ready to do.

Creating New Architecture

Just as the core choices emerged from the new architecture created by reframing, *these* choices can prompt you to *create* new inner architecture that will make these choices a reality. This naturally happens as you:
1. Identify the limiting patterns around **not** having the results you have chosen, and
2. Reframe them. Each time you reframe, you create new inner architecture.

In this approach, you are *beginning* with what you want, say, a short-term result—and *then* identifying and removing the limiting patterns that keep you from having that result. (This is an extension of the approach introduced in Chapter 6, in which you learned to work with limiting patterns connected with *not having something that you want.)*

Quick Results

This approach worked very well for Carol, a government trainer, who had been looking for over a year for a suitable housemate to share her condominium. The first day she learned this process, she applied it so fully that she found (or opened to) the right housemate *the next day.*

In this instance, the results appeared almost magical to her. However, magic, by definition, is inexplicable. That did not apply, because she *knew* how she had created this highly desired result. The only thing that had changed from one day to the next, after a year of looking for a suitable housemate, was that she had chosen to have this result and reframed the limiting patterns that stood between her and that result.

The first thing Carol did to put this result in motion, and that you can do with any result you desire, is to use the suggestions in this chapter to choose it, align with it, clear the track—and then begin applying E*ssence Repatterning* to this choice. This section will explain how to do that.

Let's go back to Helen, the client I spoke of earlier who was concerned about her husband's investment decisions. Her choice was...*to feel great about Douglas' investment decisions—and know it.* The next step in this process would be to identify, and reframe, all of the limiting patterns she could think of around the issue, starting with the most obvious ones of:

> P: *Not feeling great about Douglas' investment decisions*
>
> P: *Having a husband who makes less than optimal investment decisions*
>
> P: *Having a husband who receives/acts on less than optimal investment advice*

Choosing a New Car

But let's take the process a little deeper, in a way that can be applied to any result you want.

For example, say you want a new car (or select another result you deeply desire). Instead of simply choosing to have a new car, remember that you want to include how you feel about it. If you only choose to have a new car, you could end up with anything that's a) new, and b) is a car. By this I mean, it could be a lemon, it could be a color you wouldn't like, or a model that isn't comfortable for you, or perhaps one that has excessive monthly payments.

One way to give yourself ample room to have the result you want is to work with a choice that may be worded similarly to one of these:

> *I choose to enjoy having a new car I really love...or*
> *I choose to feel great about my new car and its low cost...or I choose to enjoy having a car that suits me to a T—and know it.*

Expediting Your Results With *Essence Repatterning*

In identifying the result you desire, and writing it down as a choice, you have taken the first step in working with this approach. Here are the basic steps to follow:

1. *Choose* the result you desire, following the suggestions in this chapter.
2. *Align* with this choice by saying:

   I choose to enjoy being in full support of and alignment with this choice and result. . . and with the choice to be receiving Optimal support for this from the Unconscious and other sources.

3. *Clear the track*— to *receive* the result you have chosen, to *have* it, *want* it, and *feel worthy* of it—by simply reframing:

   P: **Not** having a clear track to Receive this result, Have it, Want it, and Feel Worthy of it

   — Do this by saying: **I choose to reframe these patterns, and all allied limiting patterns, now and to know it.**

4. Use *Essence Repatterning* to begin identifying and removing the limiting patterns that are preventing you from having the result you desire. Start with the Five Standard Limiting Patterns.

Five Standard Limiting Patterns

To start the *Essence Repatterning* process, the most effective way to begin is by applying the Five Standard Limiting Patterns discussed in Chapter 6. They are:

- P: **Not having** the result you want
- P: **Not wanting** to have that result
- P: **Feeling unworthy** of having that result
- P: **Not doing what it takes** to have that result

P: **Telling yourself that undesirable or awful things would happen** if you **did** have that result (then identify what those things are and reframe believing these beliefs and fears)

Each of these standard limiting patterns will provoke others, layer by layer. As you begin writing them down, your unconscious will bring to mind the current layer of patterns you are ready to remove. It's important to remember that these limiting patterns don't have to make sense to you. What is important is that you write down whatever patterns you think of, or hear, or sense might be useful to reframe.

(You can even ask your friends or family for suggestions. I personally have found that sometimes others will see very obvious limiting patterns that my ego will keep hidden from me.)

If you are in doubt about whether or not a particular limiting pattern is really yours, I suggest that you include it. Why not? *You will never add a limiting pattern by doing so,* and you might remove one that is creating a blockage for you.

Ego Resistance

Of course, the ego may try to convince you that a particular pattern is certainly not yours. If there is any resistance to owning a particular pattern, it may be your ego trying to dissuade you from including a pattern that threatens it—as a way of its staying in control. In fact, I have found that resistance is a sure indication that a particular pattern is present, to some degree, anyway—otherwise, what's the big deal?

Not Having My Result

Using the choice for a new car as an example (or whatever other result you have chosen), let's start with the first fundamental limiting pattern—*not having* the chosen result—and see what some of the follow-on limiting patterns might be:

P: **Not having** *a new car I really love...*
P: *Not having the money for a new car*

P: Believing I shouldn't spend that much money on a car
P: Believing I have to spend a lot of money on a car
P: Believing that God doesn't want me to have a good car
P: Believing that I already have more than I deserve
P: Believing that I'll look too showy if I have the kind of car I really want
P: Believing that people won't like me if I have the kind of car I want
P: Believing I don't deserve to have a nice car
P: Believing I don't know how to use money wisely
P: Believing my father/mother was right—I'll never amount to anything
P: Believing I have to be like my father/mother
P: Believing I can't live any better than they did

Note: As you read these patterns, notice if they trigger any response in you. If they do, these, or similar patterns, are ones you can identify and reframe for almost any choice with which you are working.

Although the choice in this example is about a new car, the underlying patterns that would prevent one from having *any* deeply desired result probably will have a negative impact on *many* areas of one's life. As you experiment with this, you may find yourself identifying patterns that come from many surprising directions and angles. My advice to you is: Follow these pathways. Include all of these unexpected limiting patterns. Allow your unconscious to show you the patterns that you are ready to remove, whether it be with regard to a new car, job, relationship, deeper sense of inner peace, having more fun...anything you currently desire. My experience has shown that our unconscious will use whatever choices we make to help us identify the patterns that *generally* are getting in our way—both with regard to the specific result we've chosen and other aspects of our life as well.

Note: If you are feeling a bit uncomfortable, it may be because of the number and depth of patterns that you have automatically put on-line as you are learning about the process. Even if you don't want a new car, some of these limiting patterns may apply to you, or may have evoked others that apply to you. This is why it may feel a little *heavy*, or unpleasant, to you right now. That means it is probably time to reframe what has been put on-line to this point. Remember, these are only limiting patterns—and anything we can name, we can reframe. To do this, simply turn to pages 46-47, and follow the directions to do the Basic *Essence Repatterning* process by: 1) including all the permutations of each of these patterns, and 2) reframing them.

Not Wanting My Result

Now let's look at some examples of the patterns that might show up as you work with the second fundamental limiting pattern—***not wanting to have*** the chosen result. (Remember, these don't have to make sense to your logical mind. This process is showing us the patterns that are stored in the subconscious...the beliefs that hold us back.)

- P: **Not wanting** to have a new car I really love
- P: Not wanting to be seen
- P: Not wanting to show off
- P: Believing I'm a show off
- P: Believing people won't like me if I have something they don't
- P: Believing being successful means being alone
- P: Believing God didn't intend for me to be successful
- P: Believing my family will disown me if I'm too successful
- P: Believing my family will abandon me if I do it (my life) different from them

P: Believing I have to be like my family (at least to some degree)
P: Believing that people who have shiny cars are mean and nasty and have bad values
P: Believing that you can't have the good life and be spiritually sound
P: Believing that to have the good life precludes being a good, spiritual person
P: Believing that if we have a good life here, we won't go to heaven

If you are ready to reframe these patterns, turn to pages 46-47 and follow the process for doing this.

Feeling Unworthy of Having This Result

Let's look now at the limiting patterns that may arise from the third standard limiting pattern, that of *feeling unworthy of having* what you have chosen:

P: **Feeling unworthy of having** *a new car I really love*
P: Feeling unworthy of having the finer things in life
P: Feeling that I can't have what I really want
P: Believing that it's wrong to have more than others
P: Believing that it is too frivolous to have something I don't really need
P: Believing that I shouldn't get a new car until I really need it
P: Believing it is wrong to spend that kind of money on myself
P: Believing that I should only have the necessities... that I don't deserve the niceties of life
P: Believing that I will be punished if I have nice things, or things that are too nice
P: Believing that I am unworthy of presenting myself so well...and that it would be phony to do so

> P: *Believing that the best way to get by, and feel safe, is remain relatively obscure*

These may provoke other patterns for you. In fact, you may have so many on-line at this point, that it may be time to reframe them. If so, take the time to do so by following the process on pages 46-47.

Not Doing What It Takes

Now let's work with the fourth standard limiting pattern—*not doing what it takes* to have the chosen result—and see how that might play out:

> P: **Not doing what it takes** *to have a new car I really love*
> P: *Not wanting to do with it takes to have this result*
> P: *Believing it has to be hard*
> P: *Believing life has to be hard*
> P: *Believing life is a struggle*
> P: *Believing that it would be wrong if it were not a struggle...if it were easy*
> P: *Believing if I don't try, I can't fail*
> P: *Believing I have to fail*
> P: *Believing it would be wrong for me to succeed*
> P: *Believing I can't be any more successful than my father/mother*
> P: *Believing I can't be any more effective, or worthwhile, than my family*
> P: *Believing that God doesn't want me to succeed*
> P: *Believing I shouldn't succeed...that I should sabotage myself, keep my talents and strengths hidden, or at least dampened down*
> P: *Believing that the best I can do is settle for the status quo and be glad for that*

After you have added any additional patterns to your reframing list, I suggest you remove this batch before proceeding to the last standard limiting pattern—that of *telling myself that undesirable or awful things would happen if I did have the result I have chosen.* Let's see what surfaces with this pattern:

P: **Telling myself that undesirable or awful things would happen** *if I did* have the result I have chosen

P: Telling myself that I would be hurt and irreparably damaged if I was so bold as to have what I want...to really go for it

P: Telling myself that I would be severely punished if I had what I truly want

P: Telling myself that everyone would hate me

P: Telling myself that the car would be stolen...and then I'd have to get involved with the police

P: Telling myself that I wouldn't take care of it, and would probably have a terrible accident and smash it up

P: Telling myself that having a new car is too much responsibility and that I can't handle it

P: Being afraid of responsibility

P: Believing I don't have what it takes to carry my fair share in the world

P: Believing that I have to settle for small things, small results that I can handle

P: Believing I couldn't handle having the finer things in life...that I would go off-track, or go crazy

Of course, these limiting patterns could go on and on. However, it might be good to stop right here—and flesh out and reframe the patterns you've been reading and possibly writing down. To do so, follow the process on pages 46-47.

Now that you've reframed those patterns, you have a clearer track to receive that new car, or whatever result you have chosen. In fact, you have a clearer track to receive whatever you desire in general, because you've removed a substantial number of the *rules for life* you learned as a child. Of course, if the car is not showing up, it just means there are additional limiting patterns to address.

You may be asking: *How long will I have to do this?* The only honest answer to that question is: However long it takes. It will depend on what you have chosen—and the limiting patterns you have that block the result you desire.

By the way, if you did not go back and do the Basic *Essence Repatterning* process just mentioned, I suggest that you at least use the band-aid approach by reframing the specifically worded patterns that you have just read. You can do this simply by saying:

I choose to reframe these patterns, and all allied limiting patterns, now and to know it.

Note: Although using this abbreviated approach, in the moment, will *not* remove any of the other permutations of these specific patterns, as listed on pages 46-47. It will remove the barebones of the patterns you just read. This will relieve that feeling of *sluggishness* so you can move forward more comfortably with the rest of the chapter. However, I suggest that later you go back and do the whole Basic *Essence Repatterning* process on these patterns, so that you can be done with these particular patterns, once and for all.

This is essentially how you work with *Essence Repatterning* when you *start with your choice*. Once you have removed this first layer of limiting patterns regarding whatever you have chosen, you can sit down later and ask your unconscious to show you, or tell you, whatever the next layer of limiting patterns are that stand between you and your chosen result—and remove them as well. You might find it useful to begin again with the Five Standard Limiting Patterns. Each time you work with them you will see another layer of reasons why you are:

P: **Not having** the result I want

P: **Not wanting** to have that result
P: **Feeling unworthy** of having that result
P: **Not doing what it takes** to have that result
P: **Telling myself that undesirable or awful things would happen** if I did have that result *(then identify what those things are and reframe believing these beliefs and fears)*

How Important Is This Result to You?

Take a look at the choice you've been using in this example. *How important is this result to you?*

How you answer this question will determine how willing you are to stick with this process and really give it a try. Be willing to notice the changes that result, subtle and otherwise. By noticing these changes—and claiming them—you are re-educating your ego out of the status quo and into new ways. You are telling your ego that you really do want to change.

By the way, if you find yourself stuck at any point in knowing what limiting patterns are impeding your progress toward having the result you have chosen, that is a limiting pattern itself. Using the Five Standard Limiting Patterns, you might experiment with removing such patterns as:

P: Being stuck
P: Not knowing what to reframe
P: Not wanting to know
P: Not doing what it takes to know...
P: Being unclear, resistant, bullheaded, self-sabotaging... *(you get the picture)*

Once you have listed all the forms of these limiting patterns you can think of, remove them using the Basic *Essence Repatterning* process on pages 46-47.

At this point, I also would make the following choice: *to enjoy having all-encompassing clarity and vision regarding the limiting patterns that are impeding my progress toward my chosen result—and know it.*

Then I would *align* with that choice and *clear the track* for it, as discussed earlier. (This is an excellent choice to use in any situation in which you feel confused or when you simply want more clarity.)

Once you have done all this, you probably will be more available to knowing the next layer of limiting patterns that is standing in the way of the result you have chosen.

More About Choice

If you are intrigued by the concepts contained in this book and are finding them useful (or suspect that they could be if you applied them more actively), one key choice with which you might experiment is:

> *I choose to enjoy being a successful Essence Repatterner—and know it.*

Perhaps other adjectives speak more directly to you, such as choosing to be an *effective* Essence Repatterner, or *competent, proficient,* or *empowered.*

Whichever words you use, if you decide to make this choice, I suggest you also include in your choice not just *being* a successful (or whatever) Essence Repatterner, but also *feeling* and *acting* that way too:

> *I choose to enjoy being, feeling, and acting like a successful Essence Repatterner—and know it.*

Then, as with any result you desire, you can follow the process outlined in this chapter to become aligned with it and to have a clear track to receive it, etc.

Of course, there are many other life choices that you might find useful.

Through the years I have worked individually with hundreds of people in helping them identify, and word, the specific choices that are important to them. In the process, I have found that there are several basic choices that seem to evoke significant change. Included among these are choices *to enjoy being, feel-*

ing, and acting:...successful...competent...worthy...happy... effective...fulfilled...abundant...safe...at home with myself... self-trusting...peaceful...grounded...present...self-accepting... and *loving.*

Four fundamental choices that Robert Fritz has suggested in his writing are: the choices...*to be true to myself...to be free...to be healthy...*and *to be the predominant creative force in my life.*

Significant Shifts

As you apply the principles contained in this chapter to any of these and other choices you may make, you naturally will be making significant shifts in your life.

Don't be surprised if you look back a year from now, or perhaps even six months from now, and realize that, indeed, you have moved *beyond* what you could have thought was possible when you began this process.

Others *have* done it, and *are* doing it. You can, too.

Of course, if you *think you can't*, that's just a limiting pattern—and you know what to do with that!

✹ ✹ ✹

Final Note

This book represents the completion of the first phase of *Essence Repatterning* and its applications. As it goes to press, the second phase already has begun. The first phase dealt almost exclusively with work involving individuals, both in private sessions and in public seminars. The next phase will be expanded to focus more on applications within organizations and affinity groups, in which there is a common vision or goal.

Working through my company, Source Unlimited, the exclusive provider for *Essence Repatterning* consulting in an organizational setting, I have found that when this process is applied to, and by, a group of people with common goals, the results are magnified in terms of the shared vision.

Even working individually, as the only person within an organization who is doing *Essence Repatterning*, many people are experiencing significant results and changes when they begin identifying—and removing—the limiting patterns they personally experience within their organizations. I am interested in collecting written data from individuals who are using *Essence Repatterning* in this way, on their own, in their work environment, within business, government agencies, the classroom, churches, communities groups, etc.

If you are interested in learning more about *Essence Repatterning* seminars, tapes, or Practitioner Trainings, please write to the address below.

Source Unlimited
P.O. Box 15826, Chevy Chase, MD 20815

Appendix A

APPLIED KINESIOLOGY

Applied Kinesiology, also known as **Muscle-Testing**, is a method of accessing direct feedback from the body. Holistically speaking, the *body*, in this context, generally refers to the *body/mind/spirit.*

Used by many health professionals, it has been incorporated into such diverse areas as internal medicine, psychiatry, dentistry, preventive medicine, chiropractic, allergy, acupuncture, sports training, nutrition, and osteopathy, among others.

Introduced in 1964 by Dr. George J. Goodheart, it is used widely for diagnosis and determining proper treatment modalities. Its fundamental value is that it allows the practitioner to bypass the conscious mind and directly access the body's truth.

In *Applied Kinesiology* by Tom and Carole Valentine, Dr. Goodheart says: "Applied kinesiology is based on the fact that the body language never lies. The opportunity for understanding the body language is enhanced by the ability to use muscles as indicators of body language."

In evaluating the early introduction of this breakthrough technology, Dr. John Diamond, president of the International Academy of Preventive Medicine and author of *BK, Behavioral Kinesiology*, wrote: "With Applied Kinesiology, doctors had a really useful therapeutic tool, a system of feedback from the body itself. If they gave a patient the proper treatment, the body would respond immediately as if to say, 'Yes, that is what was needed.'"

Dr. Diamond, also author of *Your Body Doesn't Lie*, says that using Applied Kinesiology has also helped his patients see themselves in a new light. "Instead of submitting humbly to my treatment, they were sharing fully in it...It is an emotional experience to gain insight. And kinesiological testing is an emotional experience. It is an 'ah-ha' experience, and it is only through this kind of experience that we arrive at sudden truths."

Note: Advanced *Essence Repatterning* seminars teach participants how to muscle-test themselves and how to use muscle-testing in doing Advanced *Essence Repatterning*, which includes working specifically with *meta-patterns.*

Appendix B

Additional *Essence Repatterning*™ Experiences

• "As a psychotherapist, I believe that *Essence Repatterning* is an extraordinary breakthrough in helping individuals transform their lives. Within days of my first in-depth, individual session as a client, I noticed dramatic, positive shifts in my primary relationship. Today, just seven months later, I am experiencing love and fulfillment with my husband to a degree that previously was not possible.

"*Essence Repatterning* also has helped me let go of chronic anxieties that have plagued me for as long as I can remember. This, in turn, has helped to free up my energy, stimulate my creativity, and enrich my relationship with my son.

"Finally, using this process is revitalizing my therapy practice. As I do *Essence Repatterning* sessions with my clients, I am helping those who were previously stuck in negative self-sabotage open up new inner pathways for success and happiness in their lives."

—O.M.S., psychotherapist, Washington, D.C.

• "As a psychologist for more than 35 years, there isn't much in the way of approaches to helping people that I haven't studied, taught, practiced, or experienced. Within this context, *Essence Repatterning* is that rare experience, a refreshing breath of newness, simplicity, and effectiveness. It provides a deceptively straightforward system for making sense of the jumble of my life and of all the years and approaches I've used to try and understand it. The very idea of incorporating beliefs, actions, nonactions, thought forms, and repetitive patterns into a systematic context that gives meaning to the negative aspects of our lives is extremely helpful.

"After only a few sessions, I could see myself more clearly than I have ever done, without overwhelming guilt *and* with a knowledge that I could do something to change my self-sabotaging patterns. I have seen almost immediate results in my personal relationships. It is easy now to acknowledge what I am actually doing as opposed to what I thought I was doing in the past. My children find that to be a welcome change and are freer in expressing their real feelings about what I am or am not doing with respect to them. This is allowing my relationship with each of them to become more real and to deepen a long-developing healing process between us.

"My professional relationships are significantly improved as well. I no longer need to impress people from a limiting pattern of feeling inadequate. I have choice over my behavior now and those subtle feelings of inadequacy are changing daily into confidence. Every time I feel uncomfortable I begin to look for the implicit limiting patterns—and remove them.

"As a result of *Essence Repatterning* sessions with the staff of our non-profit organization, we now have a direction and methodology to create new tracks to allow the short- and long-term results we have chosen to manifest. Although our team has worked together for almost 10 years, and experienced many kinds of effectiveness trainings, we were still having less than optimal results, especially in terms of financial stability and consistency. We knew we needed to make some radical changes in order to move forward.

"Using *Essence Repatterning*, within an amazingly short time, it was possible to elicit a graphic picture of the first layer of limiting patterns under which we were operating. With this reference, it quickly became apparent why we were producing the limited results we were getting. Not only were we individually limiting ourselves, we were also doing it as a group. As we have progressed, layer by layer (in a very gentle process of self-discovery), we have been removing these limiting patterns—and watching the subtle and obvious changes that result."

—S.E.B., management consultant, Arlington, Va.

- "My first dramatic experience with *Essence Repatterning* occurred during an *Essence Repatterning* seminar on a lunch break with people I did not know well. At one point, one of them asked me a question and then didn't listen to my answer. In fact, as I looked around, I noticed that no one was interested in talking to me. There were a myriad of conversations circling around me, and I was part of none of them. In the past, I would have chalked this one up to a situation of being around ignorant, rude, insensitive, maybe even racist, people. In response, I considered adopting an aloof attitude or pushing my way into a conversation. As I watched all of this from an increasingly new perspective, I said to my questioner, 'You aren't listening.' Not hearing me, she continued to chat with others at the table. As I sat there, I began to realize that I, myself, was creating a sense of isolation, self-doubt, and hard feelings about people who were complete strangers—a pattern I undoubtedly had played out many times in the past, but that I never had seen so clearly. Without drawing attention to myself, I quickly used *Essence Repatterning* to remove this pattern. To my surprise, no more than a minute later, the woman next to me turned in my direction and resumed her original inquiry, while all of the others at the table focused on my response. It was as if the previous scenario of being ignored and not listened to had never happened. The dynamic at the table had completely shifted to one that included all of us.

"Since then, as I have identified and removed my limiting patterns on a daily basis, I have seen marked changes in my relationships at the hospital where I work. In the four years I have been there, it has not been a very friendly environment and I have often felt alienated. Now, when I walk through the halls, I feel a new level of connection and find myself talking with people I never would have in the past, staff and patients alike. It's amazing...almost like a fantasy. I am receiving love and appreciation in ways that I had not imagined—all of which makes my job much more rewarding.

"As I work with *Essence Repatterning*, I also am gaining more clarity about how to implement my long-term dream of helping

the general populace claim more responsibility for its health. To me, this means getting medicine and health out of the white-coat and doctor-office image, and, also, out of the health bureaucrat's hands. I am beginning to train myself in ways and means to convey and deliver the messages that will help people assume more responsibility for their individual health choices."
—R.M.J., physician, Silver Spring, Md.

Organizational Applications

As mentioned above, in addition to the application of *Essence Repatterning* with individuals in private sessions and by individuals personally, the process also is being used successfully within organizations. In that setting, the results are often magnified if the people involved are working toward a common goal.

Recent work with a Virginia-based training organization revealed limiting patterns that were *inhibiting* the principals from:
- Receiving—and seeking—necessary funding for developmental projects;
- Initiating proposals and contacts...by mainly operating from a responsive, reactive modality;
- Communicating effectively about their products and services;
- Allowing their work to reach the broadest audience it could;
- Working effectively—both individually and as a group—based upon unspoken assumptions and agreements regarding perceived roles, individual strengths, and avoiding conflict.

After one *Essence Repatterning* session in which they removed the first layer of these—and other—limiting patterns, this group reported several significant results, including:
- Receiving an unexpected, exclusive invitation to make a training proposal for a prestigious hotel chain with 150 locations in the U.S. and many more abroad;

- Communicating more naturally and effectively about their products and services in such a way that they effortlessly received a significant order in an unexpected setting;
- Hearing from a client who, for seven months, had ignored their requests to pay for a significant amount of display products, and who now wanted to clear that up;
- Receiving funding support from an organization that is in a league they had heretofore not considered.

Additional sessions with this organization have resulted in continued changes that have built upon—and expanded beyond—these changes.

Although all the results mentioned above clearly affect the bottom line, participants typically report other benefits as well. Specifically, they say that they feel more empowered, energized, and a greater sense of well-being and of being on-track. They are more confident and feel better about themselves and their ability to function effectively.

Resources Mentioned

Applied Kinesiology by Tom and Carole Valentine with Douglas P. Hetrick, D.C. (Thorsons Publishers, Inc.)

BK, Behaviorial Kinesiology by Dr. John Diamond (Harper and Row)

Do What You Love, The Money Will Follow by Marsha Sinetar (Dell)

Path of Least Resistance by Robert Fritz (Ballantine)

Three-In-One Concepts, 3210 West Burbank Blvd., Burbank, CA 91505

Your Body Doesn't Lie by Dr. John Diamond (Warner Books)